DISPATCHES FROM THE RUST BELT, VOL. VI

DISPATCHES FROM THE RUST BELT, VOL. VI

The Best of Belt Magazine 2023

Edited by Ed Simon

First Edition 2023

Belt Magazine
www.beltmag.com

Design by Meredith Pangrace

CONTENTS

GEOGRAPHY & ENVIRONMENT

MEMORY & REFLECTION

Introduction

This is a collection that I can't help but flip through with a degree of largely unearned pride. The pride is because unlike last year's collection, absolutely everything between these covers passed underneath my editorial gaze; unearned because it'd be foolish of me to pretend that my mere suggestions here or there made much of a difference improving that which is already so well done. Such is the editor's responsibility, but more importantly such is the honor of being an editor.

Within this collection you'll read about the last greyhound track in America and the queer witches of Appalachia; an account of the wealthy hobo king of St. Louis who lived a century ago and of a modern day "homeless influencer;" of an over-the-hill baseball star's return to the diamond and of the inadvertent avant-garde butter cow of the Iowa State Fair. History, culture, literature, and politics, in all of its richness, is explored in that broad space between the Alleghenies and the Mississippi, from the Great Lakes to the Ohio River, an area as confusing and contradictory, beautiful and sublime as any in the world.

Reviewing the nearly two-hundred articles that *Belt Magazine* published last year—which includes reported features, photo essays, commentary, creative nonfiction, and poetry—is a dizzying exercise in just how much talent I've been fortunate to work with over the past twelve months, but also of the richness of our region when it comes to writers. There are folks in here from Pittsburgh and Cleveland, St. Louis and Buffalo, every bit the equal of writers in New York or L.A. There is no publication like *Belt,* and I don't just say that because I'm the editor. Call our beat what you will—writing about the industrial Midwest, the Great Lakes region, northern Appalachia, the Rust Belt. I just call it good writing.

Ed Simon, *Editor*

ARTS & CULTURE

Unspooling the Cassette Tape in Springfield, Missouri

AVERY GREGURICH

There's a modern weather station on top of an old brick factory building near downtown Springfield, Missouri. At all times it calculates the relative air temperature, the wind speed, the barometric pressure, and the humidity. In the building below, many fields of science are at work, among them magnetics, physics, chemistry, and fluid dynamics. What sort of laboratory is this, and what could it possibly be producing?

National Audio Company headquarters.

Cassette tape. A lot of cassette tape.

"The audio cassette is a remarkable product. It's inexpensive, it's durable, and next to the vinyl record is the oldest format in continuous use," Steve Stepp says. He's the President of the National Audio Company, the company he and his father Warren Williams Stepp founded in 1969. In the over five decades since, the National Audio Company has weathered seismic shifts in musical formats, the internet, multiple economic recessions, and now a pandemic. Today the National Audio Company stands as one of the last places in the world making new cassette tape. "On a typical day at National Audio we manufacture between four and six million lineal feet of tape. It's all cassette tape, we don't make anything else," he says.

Along with that tape, the company also duplicates and packages cassettes for all the major music labels and over 5,000 independent labels worldwide. The NAC isn't just dabbling in a medium for hobby collectors and nostalgists: according to the entertainment data tracker Luminate, the sales of cassette tapes almost doubled in 2021 from a year prior. "During the pandemic, one of the miraculous things that happened was we returned to a point where the audio cassette and the vinyl record both outsold CDs and the commercial music market," Stepp says. "And that is something nobody would have ever bet would have happened 15 or 20 years ago."

The Duplication Room.

Some of the highest selling cassettes in the last few years were tapes made right here in Springfield, including the famous mixtape from the *Guardians of the Galaxy* film, the soundtrack for the television series *Stranger Things*, and the soundtrack cassette for *Star Wars: The Force Awakens,* one of Stepp's personal favorite projects. They are made on the same equipment, and at the same time as cassettes for small independent labels and musicians selling their tapes on Bandcamp or giving them out to friends.

"We will have anywhere from 200 to 600 music releases working in the plant at any given time. Everything goes on at one time. We kind of have a joke here: Forward In All Directions. That's our motto," Stepp says. "You just have to be you have to be too dumb to know that your business is over with and too determined to stay in it that you won't get out. We say stubbornness and stupidity as well has kept us here."

Cassettes are, and have always been, undeniably cool. In form alone they are remarkable symbols of utility, with their inexpensive construction and unassuming physical presence. They are also a crucial link to the evolution of the presentation of music in the 20th century. Carrying over some context from the vinyl record, there are two sides to an album, adding up to at most about an hour of sound which still needed to be flipped around halfway, complete with cover art and a lyrics sheet. The cassette, however, can be held in one hand, and more importantly, like the 8-track before, could be played by a tape deck in your car. It also marks the first audio medium that could be manipulated easily by an individual at home, allowing listeners to create their own cherished mixtapes and musicians to make their own recordings.

Emily Freidenrich is the author of *Almost Lost Arts: Traditional Crafts and the Artisans Keeping Them Alive* (Chronicle Books, 2019). She included Stepp and the National Audio Company's art of cassette-making along with nineteen other traditional artisans around the world, including bookmenders, globemakers, kintsugi artists, and neon sign makers.

"Cassette tapes hit that sweet spot of nostalgic, tangible objects. They are aesthetically pleasing in sound and in their neat little designed cases, but more so they require a very intentional ritual of choosing a discrete album to listen to at a time," Freidenrich says. "Meanwhile, our digital media lives conveniently on our portable devices and is infinitely streamable and perfectly programmed for the best quality…There is a slowness and imperfection to analog media that feels very human."

She sees National Audio as a small family business that has held on long enough to be put in the unique position of both the preservers and providers of the continuing legacy of audio cassettes.

"For Steve, this was a business he started with his father decades ago, originally focusing on audio books and spoken word, now carrying the whole legacy of cassette tapes onward for not just the audiophiles but also nostalgic listeners, and a new generation who are discovering cassette tapes," she says.

When National Audio Company started, Steve and his father were loading blank cartridges themselves and selling them to radio and television stations, as well as selling reel-to-reel tape to recording studios around the country. Sales representatives from various companies would visit NAC once a month, and Steve remembers the first time a representative from the Ampex Corporation showed him a cassette.

"The fella showed me a cassette and he said 'What do you think of that, Steve?' And with my usual foresight, I said, 'Well, it looks like maybe you could put that in a little doll and it would have a voice. I can't think of any other possible use for it,'" Stepp says. "And he said 'It's gonna be a little bigger than that.' And it turned out it was."

Stepp says the NAC began buying and selling tapes from small mom-and-pop shops who were making their own blank cassettes. Eventually, they couldn't supply enough cassettes to meet their demand, so they bought their first high speed automated audio cassette loader in 1980. "We thought that'll do it. We'll never need another one. That's as many cassettes as anybody will ever use," Stepp says. "And the following year, we bought two more. Then it was four more and within about five years we had 16 of those machines running." Stepp says around 30 are operating on the floor today, with 50 or 60 more kept in reserve for extra production capacity and spare parts.

By the mid-90s, with the arrival and eventual dominance of the CD, those cassette loaders slowed down a bit, but not entirely. At the time, Stepp says the NAC wasn't working exclusively in music. Instead, he says they were doing "a lot of (James) Patterson and (David) Baldacci thrillers and things like that." They also worked with the National Library Service for many years making books and magazines for the blind and visually handicapped, as well as instructional and religious material, including the Bible on tape. They themselves put a few CD duplicating machines into production, but Stepp had an intuition that cassettes weren't going to go away entirely. "We knew the CD was a miraculous new product and many people liked it, but there were more audio cassette decks than there were people in the United States, and so we knew this thing wasn't over. We got in the market with CDs for a while and duplicated those, but we knew the audio cassette had some staying power and we thought it would come back."

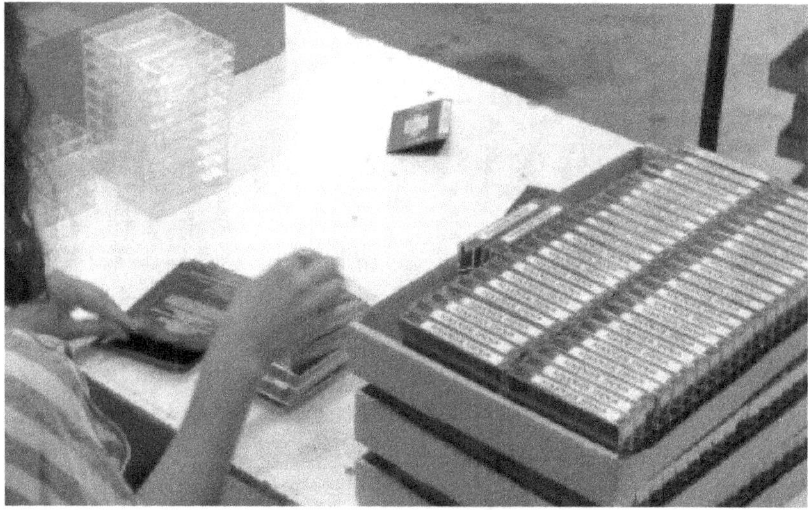

Hand packaging the Stranger Things soundtrack.

In the early 2000s, Stepp and his chief technician Bill Coverston traveled around the country with a semi-trailer, trying to buy as much cassette making equipment that they could. Oftentimes they returned home from these rescue missions with far more equipment and raw material than they had actually paid for. "We were offered a tremendous amount of just wonderful, wonderful equipment, the best that the industry has ever built at ridiculous prices. We were basically buying the equipment from them and if we hadn't bought it, it was going to go to landfills or to be sold for metal scrap. That unfortunately happened to way too many vinyl presses in the 1970s and we didn't want to see that happen to the tape equipment as well," Stepp says.

The decision to double down on that aging equipment paid off in 2009 when Pearl Jam re-released their debut album *Ten*. As part of that release, they had ordered 15,000 cassettes from NAC. Stepp says they sold out during the pre-sale and they promptly reordered thousands more. A similar project by the Smashing Pumpkins also sold thousands of cassettes, announcing to many of the major labels that had sold their equipment to the NAC just a few years before that cassettes were around to stay.

Throughout the decades, NAC has supplied cassette tape from various companies around the world. With each passing year, each one decided to get out of tape production business. In late 2016, the South Korean-based company, Saehan, that the NAC had been purchasing their tape from informed them that they were ending their tape production at the end of the year. They offered NAC the remainder of their inventory, some 300,000 reels which Stepp bought in order to give them a little time to make a tough decision. "My son and I sat down together and we said we've got to either get out of business within three years or we've got to be making tape within three years. So being sort of the stubborn sort, we decided to make tape," Stepp says. "If we hadn't done it then it could have never been done. The equipment would have been gone and we could not have afforded to ever have it built again."

Labelling cassettes.

Stepp estimates that tape hadn't been made in the United States since 1984 at the latest, so they had to scour the country for a machine able to be reconditioned back into making tape. What they found somewhere out in Nevada was a 62-foot long, 20-ton tape-coating line originally built in the 1980s that had most recently been converted into a machine for making credit card strips. They had to haul it in "across the Great Plains during a blizzard" Stepp says, and then take it apart in pieces to move it up their antiquated freight elevators, breaking one in the process. The restoration and reconditioning process took over a year-and-a-half to undergo, mostly done by people Stepp enlisted from around the country who had retired from the industry decades ago. Before our interview, Stepp was on the phone with a retired magnetic engineer trying to answer that day's question about the tape-making process.

"It was just the kindness, and there was also the fact that these guys had devoted their lives to this industry and they didn't want to see it just dry up and go away. And there was an emotional attachment, 'if I can help save this I will.' And that was a big part of it was in most cases. They had no personal gain," Stepp says. "It's a miracle that we're here. The fact that some of these people are still around and can give us their personal advice has just been invaluable. We rely a lot on the remaining knowledge of what I would call the old hands, you know, the old masters of making tape. Had we waited five more years, many of the people who were able to give us their advice would have been gone and a few of them are still around."

The machine can now produce around 20,000 feet of tape per minute amidst a tightly controlled temperature and humidity environment, hence that weather station on the top of the building. While much of this tape will fill cassettes ordered by the major labels for well-known music and television projects, some it will wind up filled with music from independent artists who order as little as 50 cassettes from NAC. Those are the ones Stepp still feels a special indebtedness to. "I tell them every time I talk to them on the phone, thank you. You guys were the lifeblood of this industry. When it didn't look like it had much blood left, it did," Stepp says. "In the end, the big guys jumped back in and said we should have never left it."

When Stepp talks about small independent labels, he is referencing music collectives like Tiny House Tapes, a cassette label based between Chicago and Milwaukee. The label began in January of 2021 when a pair of pandemic sequestered friends decided to start making and releasing cassettes. "When we started, we really wanted to do something, and I can't think of another word other than handmade," Dillon Pfau says. "Getting the J-cards printed ourselves, kind of sourcing all the materials and really trying to make it as DIY as possible. Also trying to make it as cheap as possible, mainly for the bands that we work with."

In the last two years, the label has been able to release eight cassettes from artists in both the U.S. and Canada. They have also released a pair of compilation albums of artists both on the Tiny House label and beyond. Those compilation albums were released through Bandcamp, with all proceeds being donated to The Trevor Project, a non-profit focused on suicide prevention amongst LGBTQ+ youth.

"It's definitely a passion project, not a business by any means. We both have full time jobs and are not really in this to make money," Jonah Minnihan says, who works as a manager at a bike shop in Milwaukee by day. "The way we work is we try to work with really small independent artists. We have the artists pay for all the blank cassettes and all the materials and we actually do all the work for free. So we donate all of our time to put all this stuff together, to dub it all, fit all the J-cards so that the artists that we're working with have a cheap and accessible physical format to sell at shows and give out to people or do whatever they want with."

Tape coating station.

While the pair hold some cassette nostalgia from experiencing their parents' cassettes or navigating a tape deck in their first car, they chose to start the cassette-only label for the same reasons most tape labels get started: for the format's cost efficiency, and its remarkably untouched utility.

"I think that (nostalgia) is definitely there, but I think beyond that kind of similar to the vinyl resurgence, there's almost like a different utility beyond nostalgia I think a lot of people maybe in mainstream culture kind of miss. For vinyl people, there's a lot of like audiophiles that are like 'This is the best sounding way of listening to music.' I think similarly with cassettes, the utility is maybe a bit different than fidelity. It's more about the culture around it," Pfau says. "People have been dubbing cassettes long after it's been dead. Now you can kind of find them at Urban Outfitters and stuff. I think there's a lot to be said about just the resiliency of that kind of underground culture that I've always really appreciated, and I think being a part of that has been really cool too."

Minnihan mentions a big dream of one day hosting a Tiny House Tapes concert featuring all of the artists that the pair have worked with so far. That's exactly the kind of thing possible, the gathering of performers and listeners across place and musical genre, all linked first and foremost through a beautiful and cheap plastic cassette.

There is currently a tremendous appetite from artists and consumers for new material to be released on old mediums. "Every day we have people coming to us now and saying 'Can you make VHS tape?' 'Can you make floppy disks?' 'Can you make this or that?' And the truth is, the answer to that is yes," Stepp says. He says their tape-making machine could be reconditioned to make practically any of these older formats, if given the right demand and the time with which to do it. This collective nostalgia for cassette tapes and other earlier mediums feels warranted in response to a future that looks to be filled with continuing societal injustice, extremist political violence, and natural disaster. If nothing else, the cassette tape might be the last truly safe refuge from insatiable and increasingly pervasive advertisers and exploitative streaming platforms.

As for the National Audio Company, Steve Stepp promises that NAC will be around until the very last cassette is made. At the start of every tour that he does, he says that "if you're an analog person, you have just arrived at Valhalla as the Vikings say."

And at the conclusion of the tour, he tells people: "Get a good look. You will never see this again."

"I don't think that's an exaggeration," he says. "You will never see this again."

Trent Reznor's Conflicted Rust Belt Legacy

CASEY TAYLOR

They closed the Reznor plant in 2019, but it was called Nortek by then. It closed a little more than a hundred years after George Reznor wandered back to his favorite place–the porch of the Reznor mansion in Mercer, PA–and allowed his brilliant mind to finally stop creating lightning. That day was spent like many others, according to the Mercer Dispatch in September of 1911, conversing with "comrades" in the town square of the thriving southwestern Pennsylvania economy that formed around one of his many innovations: a gas stove that would help his neighbors cook and stay warm during the cold Appalachian nights, where pockets of snow were dumped by God when the air from His rivers and lakes collided. The whirring of the machines fell silent, but the high pitched squeals and grinding metal would embed itself in the DNA of the Reznor name, such that George's great great grandson would change the world of music forever. But these things take time, and Trent Reznor was barely on the mind of the Creator when George was cooking up new ideas to improve his neighbors' lives.

George died about fifty years before the Reznor Manufacturing company was sold in 1963. It was about twenty years after the Johnstown Flood, when the shoddily constructed playground for wealthy industrialists like Andrew Carnegie that was the South Fork Hunting and Fishing Club's lake collapsed and drowned the working class living in the valley below. The Flood killed more than 2,000 people in 1889, just one year after Reznor founded his manufacturing company, and the survivors were unable to recover monetary damages from the wealthy who were responsible for the catastrophe. Instead, the Flood became the first major disaster relief effort, focused on blaming and preparing the citizenry for the danger of the elements instead of remedying the fact that a small handful of people had the money and power to drown thousands through institutions established for the wealthy's pursuit of leisure. The government changed the laws after that so you could sue people who killed your family and buried all of your possessions underwater, assuming you had the money and education to hire a lawyer that wouldn't take advantage of you.

The Rust Belt has never been big on subtlety, and it hasn't cared much about time since the 1980s. When the City of God collapses, time flattens as the aspirations of an entire population deflate, and the only way to mark the time is to pass the monuments to the Extraordinary Men like George Reznor in the dilapidated factories up for auction or the antiques floating around southwestern PA. In the lobby of the Reznor plant, now "Nortek," there was a display of the ancient pre-1950s gas stoves, a reminder that our best ideas could always just get bought out from under us instead of providing long term comfort.

And Reznor was *the* Extraordinary Man. An engineer who took up studying medicine as a hobby because of a lively mind, Reznor joined the Mercer Rifles as an infantry volunteer in the Civil War, later dubbed the 10th Pennsylvania Reserve Regiment, killing Confederates all over Pennsylvania and Maryland. Once his service finished, Reznor went ahead and invented entirely new methods of processing gas and eventually the aforementioned stove that would create an entire economy. In his spare time, he founded a school in Mercer to take care of the orphans created when hundreds of men in the 10th Reserve died during the War.

By any and all measures, Reznor was deserving of his status in the community, but this success blinded future generations to its shaky foundation. Reznor may have been the inventor and the manufacturer, but he wasn't the money man. The money men in Western Pennsylvania are the recognizable names that are now plastered on banks and universities across the region, Ulster Scots like the Mellon Family that were Irish and Scottish in name only, allied with the greater wealth of the United Kingdom and loyal to Britain. Ulster-Scotts were largely Presbyterians–a faith heavy on neighborly duties but light on patience for deviations from the norm–so that Andrew Carnegie's pamphlet *The Gospel of Wealth* sought to justify excess and wealth building as a means of shielding that same capital reserve from those whom the industrialist felt were incapable of managing such wealth. But who then are the good guys again? The guys killing laborers in the street to make steel as cheaply as possible? It's hard to keep track in an algorithmic and scientific society, where collateral atrocity is an ingredient in a man's legacy rather than a dealbreaker.

The men who commission the histories are always the good guys. That's not a novel observation, but it's worth wondering just how much those histories embed themselves into our collective unconscious—not in any supernatural sense, but in the billions of nanoseconds spent observing the material remnants of colossal failure while being fed the same lies your ancestors believed. People like Carnegie, the American Scotsman to beat all American Scotsman, now no longer the indentured servants to the crown of Britain. Rather, they were had become the independently wealthy industrialists who colonized the Appalachians and built their own society in the vision of the Presbyter. Andrew Carnegie was no Ulster Scot—one of the rare Rags to Riches stories that isn't bullshit—but he has a retroactive reputation as the most PR savvy of all the industrialists. His story was repeated in pamphlets and newspapers to help reinforce this idea of the American Dream, all of which helped to run cover for the Mellon families of the world. The independently wealthy who hid behind Carnegie's story of achievement to create an aura of "we're all in this together" solidarity.

It's a contributing factor for why the Rust Belt's relationship to race is so complicated—why it's at once tangibly racist while holding some of the most sacred abolitionist history in America's records. Up and down Appalachia people were fed the same liberation theology that inspired John Brown to raid Harper's Ferry, but they were also getting cut in on a zero sum economy. The theology worked on those who operated the Underground Railroad routes through West Viriginia and up into Mount Washington in Pittsburgh, but most of the white people did what European whites have always done do in those situations - they cut Black people out.

That spirit of rebellion has existed long before the Industrial era, though. The Appalachians, in many ways, haven't been the same since the Whiskey Rebellion. The frequency of liberation can never be fully muted, emanating from deep within the bosom of the mountains, likely formed sometime back when it was still part of the Caledonians in the center of Pangaea. But the descendants of the wealth generated by Ulsters (whether Presbyterian or Episcopalian) blew up the Hill District, not Shadyside, and it's wise to internalize the reasons rather than brush it off as yet another historical example of callous racism. Like the Ulsters before them, the Scotch Irish didn't organize along class lines and many were still loyal to the world's most overzealous imperial project in Britain. That was where the money and comfort came from.

George Reznor, like Carnegie before him, was the salt of the Earth stand-in to cover for the wealthy leeches who built a Ponzi scheme to draft off of his invention. His descendants cashed in when they sold the company in 1963 to ITT Inc., a manufacturing corporation out of upstate New York that was founded as International Telephone & Telegram. Among other various white-collar horrors that defined early corporate life, ITT had a remarkably close relationship with the Third Reich, though it's hard to say how much of Nazi money was used in any acquisition, given that Hitler had long fallen by the time Mercer, Pennsylvania was sold from underneath its own citizens. Offshoring to Belgium started a year later in 1964.

George's great grandson, a musician of some renown f, Michael Trent Reznor, was born in 1965 and after his parents divorced ended up living with his grandparents in the same town that was still bleeding to death from a wound that his father and aunts and uncles opened. From that experience, Reznor would go on to be the primogeniture of the appropriately named genre of industrial music, most famously explored in his seminal band Nine Inch Nails.

Trent Reznor's upbringing was pleasant, and most of the existential and nihilistic dread he discussed while doing press for his second album, *The Downward Spiral*, was based on seeing images of thriving success in mass media while surrounded by a stagnant rural community. The Reznors had no reason to view themselves as part of the problem, at least not one that was readily apparent. They were makers, descended from a truly Great Man whose mind likely improved countless lives in his generation and the many that came after. They didn't ask for the economy to collapse. They didn't ask for the corporation that took money from the Third Reich to offshore production to Belgium and guarantee that within a few short decades the families that had previously been indebted to the Reznor mind–knowingly or unknowingly–would end up drowning in the filth left by the wake of its commodity price.

The Flood comes for all, but a flood is quick and loud. A drought is so much more effective at killing people without anybody noticing, because a drought is a compounded tragedy that develops slowly. A drought manipulates peoples' most base instincts, like the fear of hunger or death. Nobody can stop a drought. If a drought is nothing more than the loss of an essential source of abundance, a drought can be a closed factory, which leads to slowed commerce, which leads to foreclosed houses, which leads to a host of complications of human behavior. We're animals, after all, and animals may be able to learn helplessness, but they never forget to try and survive.

The stories of the Depression aren't history for the people of Appalachia, but a recognizable frame of reference for the people whose aunts and uncles still stand in bread lines; the people who have a relative that starved to death in the bosom of abundance. Mercer and New Castle Pennsylvania are as much a Ground Zero as anywhere else on this side of the Appalachians, the sheen of prosperity from the East Coast slowly fading as one gets closer to Ohio Valley. These things take time, and collapse is felt before it can fully manifest. George's great-grandson was pretty honest about that in interviews in the 1990s, a fallen prince of the Rust Belt colonizer class; the new Ulster Scots, ripped from the Highlands playbook, now left to watch as the utopia they were promised turned to ash.

Trent Reznor's work as Nine Inch Nails stands out amongst other industrial metal acts—a genre that fused the UK's Industrial scene with the hissing screeches of machines reminiscent of an assembly line sped up to the point of combustion. Nine Inch Nails work was remarkably personal compared to the other innovative industrial music echoing from the hollowed-out livelihoods of the Rust Belt. The rest of the genre was far more subversive; Reznor found a way to break through on the radio, but bands like Ministry had already been creating audio and visual art meant to shock the proletariat who engaged with it. Industrial music for an industrial civilization; a tongue-in-cheek dare to its listeners to face their complicity in fascism. Reznor's work does that as well, but requires a level of self-awareness to spot it: the narrator is you, and the resonance comes from the fact that every urge he sings about, no matter how perverse, is recognizable.

Starvation in the Appalachians in the 20th century or drowning in the 19th century always comes back to the same excuse: an unavoidable calamity, or natural outcome of how things break sometimes. Never an assessment of the system that created it. Never an honest appraisal of the ways that our colonial instincts continue to manifest regardless of domestic versus international designation. If somebody in Mercer starves to death because of imperialist capital or a Cuban kid gets flayed by a paramilitary we fund, that's collateral damage. This should sound familiar to anyone with a keen eye towards the way private equity has squeezed everyone in the United States and made it even harder to acquire ownership stake in a piece of the world you're meant to improve.

Trent Reznor never mentioned the Johnstown Flood in his interviews on MTV, though he would've learned about it the same way any other Rust Belt boy does. He never mentioned the Ulster Scots and Anglo aristocrats that loaded his family with money and made them believe they were the kingmakers–until reminding them who God really was when He seized all their prosperity from across an ocean. He never mentioned the Nazis that helped the ITT corporation build on its immense capital reserves. He never mentioned that he was a rich boy surrounded by a world his ancestors got tricked into helping destroy, maybe because he was raised far away from it after his parents divorced and he moved back to Mercer from Ohio.

Yet, a hundred years after the Johnstown Flood drowned the lower classes, Trent Reznor released "Head Like a Hole," the song that would catapult Industrial music into the forefront of post-New Wave experimentation. The lyrics of Pretty Hate Machine are personal enough that they can apply to just about anyone going through a crisis, but in the context of the Tower of Babel having already collapsed around Trent's own last name, there's little else it could be about to a Southwestern Pennsylvania boy. The song that created pop nihilism could've only come from the Rust Belt, where the Ulster Scot Method drained even the rich kids of their will to live. And there are still some who would deny He has a sense of humor.

Unlocking the Gateway to the West

EILEEN G'SELL

"People who live by rivers dream they are immortal."
~ Audre Lorde, "St. Louis a City Out of Time," 1971

As the sun set over the Fulda river on Juneteenth, 2022, the Philadelphia-based practice Black Quantum Futurism performed before a dazzled crowd in Kassel, Germany. Two of hundreds of contributors to *documenta 15*, Camae Ayewa and Rasheedah Phillips stood on "The Clepsydra Stage" (2022), devised of two floating circular clocks that move with the river current, their voices ricocheting off the banks in anthemic lyricism. "To submerge the Master's clock," Ayewa intoned, "is a revolutionary act within a revolutionary act of escape." I was in the enviable, if lonely, position of visiting Kassel for the first time by myself, a peripatetic, porous person roving around the Hessian town in search of meaning—or art. Whichever came first.

Jump forward a year and almost five thousand miles away, and the Afrofuturist duo sets the clock to CDT in my hometown. Part of the second installment of St. Louis's Counterpublic triennial, *SLOWER-THAN-LIGHT SHRINE: IN REMEMBRANCE OF THE UNDERGROUND RAILROAD* glints from a grassy lot a block west of Jefferson Ave. Shaped in the likeness of a Kongo cosmogram, a core symbol in Bakongo spirituality, the shrine is assembled out of wrought-iron gates, archways, and lattices salvaged from demolished homes in the area. Afro picks, conk shells, broken glass, and skeleton keys adorn the metal structure; mirrors and antique time pieces affixed to its layered surfaces reflect the summer sun, snagging the eye of passersby in this quiet urban enclave. While the supplemental text explains that the piece is meant to pay tribute to "liberation seekers who traversed the Underground Railroad in St. Louis, using the caves beneath the city on their path," the monument feels more an homage to the dignity of the Black St. Louis community through decades of systematic displacement and disenfranchisement.

SLOWER-THAN-LIGHT SHRINE is but one of twenty-five sites on view till July 15th, most on view in public space, with internationally renowned contributors like Torkwase Dyson, David Adjaye, and Jaune Quick-to-See Smith, alongside regionally notable artists like Damon Davis, Yvonne Osei, and Katherine Simóne Reynolds. Whereas Counterpublic 2019 seemed to most overtly prioritize the vantage of curator and co-founder James McAnally, in this year's iteration, a diverse array of curators, artists, and St. Louis communities lead the way. Critically, of the thirty artists included, almost all are of Black or indigenous descent—and some, like Davis, were raised in poverty and have firsthand knowledge of the structural violence of St. Louis's history of racial segregation. Also distinct from 2019, several of the works onsite—like Adjaye's public earthen sculpture, *Asaase III*, adjoining the Griot Museum of Black History—are permanent.

Like the recent *documenta*—from its cadmium yellow signage to its advised engagement with public space—of which the most compelling works, in my view, unsettled their nondescript settings, the most powerful parts of Counterpublic 2023 fruitfully disrupt Jefferson Avenue, the major north-south thoroughfare that has served as a border between the city's downtown center and the westward migration (or forced expulsion) of its citizens. While nearby districts like South Grand and Washington Ave are mostly gentrified, Jefferson itself is not; outside adjoining neighborhoods like Lafayette Square, Benton Park, and the Cherokee Arts District, it is pocked with civic neglect. I have driven it numberless times and never walked the grounds of most of the installations on view at Counterpublic. Walking north and south this summer, I discovered—strike that, encountered—spaces that I had not known existed. I was hot. I was sweaty. And more crucially, I was humbled.

Unlike *documenta*, most Counterpublic installations were created by individual artists, rather than collectives, though the exhibition overall retains a collaborative feel built from the efforts of the four curators—New York's Diya Vij, Chicago's Allison Glenn and Risa Puleo, and the indigenous group New Red Order—who joined local curators and communities in the process of conceptualizing and realizing the event.

In the north hub off Jefferson, Torkwase Dyson's immersive architectural and sonic installation *Bird and Lava (Scott Joplin)* stands in the south of St. Louis Place Park. Open to all 24/7, the simultaneously sun-dappled and cavernous space proves both a perfect spot for a picnic or pensive contemplation. Stepping up into a circular door to the west, the structure resembles a minimalist portal to another world. And it is. As Joplin's ragtime tunes float from the speakers lining the inner walls, the venerable trees, houses, and churches in the vicinity throb with its syncopations. We are reminded of not only Joplin, but so many Black creatives for whom the city was once home—Josephine Baker, Chuck Berry, and Tina Turner among them.

Heading south on Jefferson toward the southwest entrance of CITYPARK, the soccer stadium at Jefferson and Market opened in 2022, an imposing cluster of eight granite sculptures tower over both the curious and oblivious. Named for the Mill Creek Valley neighborhood in which twenty thousand Black St. Louisans resided in the first half of the twentieth century, and on which the stadium now stands, Damon Davis's *Pillars of the Valley* calls attention to the mass erasure and displacement conducted in the name of "urban renewal." Next to the pillars, contextualizing the larger history of the space, a vast stone map reveals how massive the area once was—some 450 acres— and how few of its former sites still remain. Part of the Great Rivers Greenway Brickline Project that, upon completion in 2030, will join ten miles of trails connecting fourteen predominantly Black St. Louis neighborhoods, *Pillars of the Valley* will eventually stretch a mile long to mark the boundary of the Mill Creek Valley district. "It was a joy," reads one quote from a former Mill Creek resident, engraved on a pillar's surface. "I grew up joyfully."

A few blocks south, Jefferson Avenue Bridge extends a half mile over an industrial terrain of train tracks and forklifts, the median strip and ends of the bridge under serious construction. When I arrived on foot after parking my car at the nearby QuikTrip, a light rain had just cleared; the sky was electric with loitering clouds, the setting sun streaked with peach. Strewn colorfully across the half mile of pavement, Yvonne Osei's *While You're Still Here* confronts the viewer with verdant vinyl florals, each end of the bridge depicting a female worker in the area, her face and body bedecked in blooms. Below a splash of sunflowers peeking through a crack in the concrete lie a discarded pack of Newports, a bag of cheddar puffs, and a sodden baby diaper. Together, they seemed to suggest that, even in what seems a desolate space, new life grows. Someone was *here*.

As a city of erstwhile national prominence (the national capital almost moved here in 1869), St. Louis has long been understood as a metonym for urban decline. My city has also not been particularly adept at acknowledging its sins, past or present, let alone attempting to atone for them. Counterpublic cannot redress centuries of racism, fear, and ignorance, but it can—and does—at least bring to (sometimes bitter, often unflattering) light the scars that the city's Black, brown, and indigenous communities have endured, along with the healing that need take place in time, over time, if we are to share a future. Next to the car wash on 2311 Jefferson another half mile south, Simiya Sudduth's vibrant *Justice* mural reimagines the tarot card as a red-gowned woman holding two bolls of cotton. *Are we in the South*? one might ask, facing the signature red brick that characterizes most of the city's residential buildings. Are we ever.

Growing up in St. Louis in the 80s and 90—eldest daughter of a letter carrier and a stay-at-home mom, both white and both college educated, if economically lower income—I saw myself as the natural heir to a can-do, pioneering spirit epitomized by the Gateway Arch, Eero Saarinen's modernist flex completed in 1965, when my father was eleven years old. My school teachers called us "Midwestern," never Southern, and with the lack of conspicuous twang in their timbre, I never questioned it. Our school books taught us of the Missouri Compromise and Dred Scott decision, but never of vicious red-lining policies, the neglect and ultimate collapse of Pruitt-Igoe, or the "Sundown Towns," like Ferguson, in which Black people could not be safe in public if the sun had set. Everything southern about us could be conveniently abstracted, distanced. Counterpublic does the opposite.

Continuing south on Jefferson Ave, after passing the street I lived in as a child (Miami, which, as a toddler, I called "your Ami," misconstruing the word's syntax), and then street after street named for an Indian nation (Chippewa, Keokuk, Osage…), Counterpublic's southern-most tip, Sugarloaf Mound, is honored for what it is: the oldest human-made structure in St. Louis and the last intact Native American mound in a city that was once called "Mound City." Nestled beside a tiny white house in which, I learned during the press tour a tiny white lady with a tiny white dog has lived all her life, the sacred burial mound is bordered by chain-link fence; no one would know it was there unless told in advance. Above Sugarloaf, a billboard designed by New Red Order announces, "This Billboard Is on Sacred Land"; its flipside, by Anna Tsouhlarakis, reads, "When You Listen, the Land Speaks." Below, Anita and Nokosee Fields's forty colorful wooden platforms dot the grass, designed in accordance with Osage symbolism. "What does a native future look like?" a yellow sign asks from a telephone pole. And how can we know without knowing the past?

Two blocks east of Jefferson, rising two hundred feet above 20th St, at the edge of where Mill Creek Valley once pulsed with life, The St. Louis Wheel at Union Station is perhaps the most unconventional space for productive disruption: a selection of the gondolas features *Sky is the Only Roof*, a sound installation from Steffani Jemison made in collaboration with Jackie and Glen "Papa" Wright. As the giant Ferris wheel levitates above the city—illustrious downtown to the east, light industrial to the west—the 1954 erasure of this once thriving Black community is more potently visible than on the ground. To the east: historic edifices, parks, and landmarks bear the patina of having survived for decades, if not centuries. They have personality, a soul. To the west: ghosts of what, as Jemison recites between the ting of a triangle and the tremble of cymbals, were once beloved theatres, hotels, cafes, and clubs, all of which are now endless parking lots or anonymous warehouses. Percussion explodes after Jemison's sobering enumeration; birdsong flits thereafter.

"Our City Our Spirit" declares the banner draping the side of the new professional soccer field. No doubt spirits dwell here. But are we as a city ready to claim them?

Carrie Furnace's Blood, Sweat, and Fire

EMMA RIVA

While being driven back from the airport, my cab driver told me that his parents used to let him watch bits of hot metal slush into the Monongahela like fireworks. I think of the bits of molten steel glimmering against my cab driver's grey river as "Pittsburgh fireworks."

In Pittsburgh poet Ron Gavalik's *Slag River Sins,* he describes a similar experience of watching that industrial process with his father, a hard-drinking union man whose most solemn introspections emerged when witnessing the strange beauty of the steel industry's destructive relationship with the surrounding nature. Gavalik's father ascribes power to the slag, an ability to wash away the sins of the past, even if his heart is too hardened to speak those past transgressions out loud. Kristofer Collins, another native son of Pittsburgh, writes in "Poem for Michael Wurster" from *Roundabout Trace:* "Since then I have climbed the shadowy bulk / of Carrie Furnace, imagined the deafening blaze, / and took note of each weed now sprouted / where the heavy-shod feet of lonely men / pressed a signature of sorts into the poisoned ground."

Writer and scholar Michael Wurster once said that everyone should write a poem about a steel mill. These hulking behemoths with their slag and hot metal are rarely described as beautiful, but yet I am drawn to them over and over again. My theory is that the rush of dopamine human beings get from watching fire and coal derives from our proximity to danger, death, and destruction. I certainly felt that at the Festival of Combustion held on the site of the former Carrie Furnace in Swissvale, Pennsylvania last October. I watched an older man show his kids how to run their hands along the smooth end of a knife so as to feel the metal without getting hurt. I roasted marshmallows over a display of flaming ingots reading *FINE WITH THIS.* I watched fire mold things and melt them and turn them to dust. These fires were manmade, but I still got the sense of witnessing something primal and uncontrollable that dares human beings to try to tame the flames we create.

The Festival of Combustion is sponsored by Rivers of Steel, the Homestead-based nonprofit organization that manages Carrie Furnace as a historic site. Prior to attending the Festival, I'd only seen Carrie Furnace as a hulking metal shape on the horizon over The Waterfront, an outdoor shopping center across the river, which is itself situated on the grounds of a former steel mill. Rather than the Carrie site having been turned into a mall, however, and Rivers of Steel worked to preserve the site so that events like the Festival of Combustion could be held on its grounds.

The experience of the furnace is almost indescribable. Going there feels like being on a pilgrimage. I traveled on foot from the bus stop and walked down a winding road of clover and milkweed and goldenrod growing alongside the gravel. I watched the rollercoasters and rides of nearby Kennywood disappear over the curve of a hill as I trekked down the dirt road to the furnace. Currants grew up along the barbed wire separating the road from the empty field of grass, tiny red berries like pinpricks of blood. The furnace is a testament to the balance between a celebration of human innovation and the cost of our dominion over nature.

I got to the Festival just as the heavy metal band World II were finishing their set, which the lead singer shared was their very first show. It had never occurred to me until that very moment that "heavy metal" had a meaning broader than just music. I listened to the thrum of the guitars and crash of the drum in a Judas Priest cover in the presence of a site of *literal* heavy metalworking. Rivers of Steel president Augie Carlino took the stage afterwards to welcome everyone to the "magnificent" revival of the Festival after its two-year hiatus. "This site has always been commemorative of the industrial history of Pittsburgh that you see all around, and to remind everyone who talks about 'new' technological development in our city that it isn't that new. We're fortunate to live somewhere that celebrates innovation," he said. Carrie Furnace serves as a reminder of how volatile the boom and bust of that innovation is, long before Google and Duolingo, and the Festival of Combustion is a crie de coeur to remember that the human beings that build technology are more important than the technology itself.

And even with all this waxing poetic, I came because I wanted to see things getting set on fire. Shortly after my arrival, I headed for the blacksmithing demonstration tent, which was where I met bladesmith Jared Ondovchik of Artifact Metalworks. As he "quenched" an orange molten knife in water, he mused: "There are myths about blacksmiths that they used to quench their knives in blood instead of water. I used to think that was bullshit, but you think about what people do to each other and it's kind of believable." He then gave a big belly laugh and stuck the knife back in the flame.

Ondovchik is deeply dedicated to metalworking, explaining that "nothing easy is ever simple" about his craft. Even the everyday tools that we use in our kitchens, or gardens, or basements are the products of complex artistry. The same applies to everything that makes up the network of human life, including the streets we walk and the houses we live.

I stood around with Ondovchik and the other onlookers, who had come all the way from Phoenix, Arizona, and talked about metalworking and weapons. I've always related to people with an affinity for the craft making and artistry behind weapons. I was a former competitive fencer in the weapon of épée, which is modeled after dueling swords, and Ondovchik grew up around firearms in rural Aliquippa. Like the fire used to make them, the weapons we forge gives us a proximity to destructive power. There's something incredibly spiritual about creating something with the power to harm, and it makes one think about how everything we create, not just knives and swords and guns, carries that potential harm.

Ondovchik's demonstration celebrated the time and care it took to make a tiny knife with a delicate spiral on its handle. "A lot of blacksmithing is preserving the ancient craft," he said. "Sometimes the process forces me to explore and improve." The presence of the furnace in the background brought to mind questions about labor and creation, and the paradox that while hard work is the easiest to exploit, sometimes it can also be the most rewarding.

As the sun started to set, local band Bindley Hardware Company began a cover of Johnny Cash's classic "Ring of Fire." If any lyrics could ever capture the paradox of creation and destruction in flames, the contradiction of the blood, sweat, and ash that goes into creating something, it would be June Carter Cash's half-lament and half-love song to the intoxicating power of desire.

The Festival celebrates how fire hurts, inspires awe, and fear whether the burn of whiskey in our throats is from Knob Creek Distillery or the burning bush in Amy Foster's egg tempera paintings. The history of our region is one of baptisms and deaths by fire. I haven't written a poem about a steel mill yet, but as I watched the flames of an iron pour solidify at the foot of Carrie Furnace, I knew I'd already fallen into western Pennsylvania's ring of fire.

Bow Before the Butter Cow

MILES MACCLURE

Some teachers spend their summers hiking, swimming, and road tripping, but one devotes her summer to sculpting the annual butter cow for State Fairs. Butter sculpting, for the uninitiated, is exactly what it sounds like; the practice of piling, carving, and chiseling copious amounts of butter into the desired sculptural form. Sarah Pratt, a special education teacher from Iowa, began apprenticing as a butter sculptor at the age of 14, and hasn't looked back since. Pratt accompanied a friend to the 1991 Iowa State Fair 4-H competition, and after botching several tasks, found herself relegated to carrying buckets to the back room, where she encountered her future mentor, Norma 'Duffy' Lyon, crafting that year's edition of the butter cow. This encounter sparked over a decade of butter sculpting apprenticeship under Norma before taking over lead sculpting duties in 2006. Every summer, Pratt crafts the butter cow in her home state of Iowa, and travels to Illinois and Kansas to create their respective State Fair butter cows.

The long running state fair tradition of butter sculpting can be traced back to the 1903 Ohio State Fair, first appearing at the Iowa State Fair in 1911, and Illinois in 1922. This year's Iowa exhibition featured a marriage proposal and Illinois' cow was revealed in a ceremony featuring Governor J.B. Priztker.

The 2022 Illinois State Fair butter sculpture features a life size dairy cow clutching a sunflower between its teeth and a boy kneeling on the ground next to the cow, his arms outstretched and hands caressing the base of a sunflower growing in the butter-ground. The center of the sunflower is adorned with the words 'grow with us', the theme of this year's state fair and the inspiration for Sarah Pratt's inclusion of sunflowers in the sculpture. A second sunflower in the ground features the logo for Undeniably Dairy, a dairy resource for farmers. The fragile and ephemeral nature of the sculpture becomes palpable as the rotating pedestal halts and the cow's slender tail wobbles on the brink of detachment. Contrary to what one might expect, the hundreds of pounds of butter shaped into a cow does not project sentiments of excess or gluttony, but rather an unusual sort of awe.

Sarah Pratt's sense of connectedness with the earth and grounding appreciation of the nourishment provided by cows and farmers was clear when I spoke to her by phone. She speaks with such care and commitment to her craft, intent on keeping alive a tradition carried by her mentor, Norma, for over thirty years before Pratt took the helm. Pratt mentions the butter sculptures as an opportunity for children to learn lessons in ephemerality and impermanence by putting forth time and effort into a structure that ultimately lasts for such a brief moment.

Pratt maintains commitment to the materiality of butter by refraining from putting any additives or color into the butter. "There was something lost in the use of color that made it feel not like butter anymore. And so, there's this balance for me to be authentic to the sense that this is butter," she says.

Crafted in a mere seven days, the sculpture is composed of over 500 pounds of butter that's been recycled each year for over ten years running. Pratt tells me the butter becomes increasingly dehydrated over time, which makes the butter easier to sculpt with. Formal aesthetic questions linger about some sculptural choices; if the boy is supposedly planting the sunflower, then why are his hands cupped around the stem several inches above the ground, and why would he be planting a flower that has already bloomed? Given Pratt created the sculpture in a week, the level of detail is nothing short of impressive, one can only speculate what she might be able to accomplish with a longer timeframe.

The 2022 Illinois State Fair Butter Cow is housed within a polygonal industrial refrigerator, the cow itself stands on a rotating pedestal in the lineage of rotary pie displays and automobile turntables, its elevated stature and aptly lit display booming out to say, that *"This is what you came to see."* Windows adorn all sides of the display unit, perfect for facilitating the slightly uncomfortable moment of you catching me looking at you looking at the butter cow. One can press their nose up against the glass to get closer, although layers of muck and condensation accumulated from several years' worth of state fairs cloud the view, not to mention the pool of liquid leaking from the refrigeration. The lack of pristine presentation conditions isn't to denigrate the artwork by any means, and I'm not convinced the work would be improved by viewing it through Windex polished windows. If the presentation of the artwork is intended to mirror the conditions of the thing it represents, then we must go with the fact that barns and dairy facilities are far from pristine, the imperfections are what make the artwork compelling, and no one in the audience seems to mind the refrigeration coolant pooling on the ground. If eight bay windows and a rotating pedestal aren't enough viewing perspectives, a downward 45-degree angle is available via the Butter Cow Webcam livestream on the Illinois State Fair website. Precisely why there is a livestream of the butter cow remains somewhat of a mystery.

While visiting the cow in person, the level of engagement between fellow viewers and the cow was high. The room was filled with wide eyes and excited chatter; parents, children, the elderly, and everyone in between expressed equal excitement while looking at the cow, and people stayed for much longer than the average person stares at a Rothko painting in a museum. Even prior to setting foot in the dairy building, I overheard chatter about the butter cow throughout the fairgrounds. At the entry to the building that houses the butter cow is a cow sculpture made from metal. No one stopped to look at it.

Hidden in the sculpture are thirteen hearts in reference to the thirteen essential nutrients found in milk, a detail Pratt began adding to each sculpture a few years ago as an extension of her family tradition of collecting heart shaped rocks. Hidden throughout are small hearts representing calcium, vitamin d, riboflavin, phosphorus, protein, potassium, vitamin a, vitamin b12, niacin, pantothenic acid, zinc, selenium, and iodine. While the practice of adding vitamin D to milk, which began in the 1930s, certainly appears to be a good thing, I'm mildly incensed that one of the nutrient hearts nestled in the butter cow is there because it's artificially added to dairy products. If there's anything more American than a cow sculpted from butter, it's the use of technicalities to bend the truth to do one's bidding. Granted, the infraction at hand is a minor one, and surely no ill will was meant by informing fairgoers that Vitamin D can be consumed by drinking milk, but I just can't shake the sour taste of learning the nutrient information is somewhere west of the truth, although more things likely fall into this category than we care to admit.

This is supposedly an article and review of the 2022 Illinois State Fair Butter Cow, crafted by the esteemed butter sculptor Sarah Pratt. It is, and has been that, but it is also a reminder, at the very least for myself, that the art one looks at is not always for oneself.

There's a large swath of participants in the contemporary art world who likely have little interest in butter cow sculptures, or for that matter, any artwork that requires wading through a sea of corn dog stands and a dense cotton candy air in order to reach the viewing room. There's no butter cow NFT and it won't be on view at Art Basel this year; it's a Springfield, Illinois exclusive. I mention this contemporary art world because I'm a part of it and have firsthand witnessed art viewers (including myself) swiftly dismiss an artwork they don't understand, often when it comes from a culture foreign to them, or one perceived as being of a supposedly lesser sophistication. I've spent a good deal of time stewing over holes to melt in the butter cow, fact-checking nutritional information. And for what end?

Looking at art, and making art, are often solitary activities, which often render them as selfish pursuits which take the form of objects that reflect larger cultural trends, concerns, and cultural goods serving the public interest. This dynamic, however, leads to situations where the art looker becomes upset when they view an artwork they cannot comprehend. ("This isn't art!") How could the all-knowing, sophisticated art looker, fail to comprehend the significance and purpose of the artwork in front of them? Surely, they're up to date on all information required to understand all artwork of relevance to them.

I'm fascinated by the butter cow, I'm in deep admiration of the butter cow, I'm in full support of butter cows to be sculpted for years to come, but I can't claim to fully understand the butter cow. Does it matter that the sculptural details veer towards the uncanny, or that there's a heart for an artificially added nutrient? Perhaps I don't understand the butter cow because I'm trying to understand the butter cow. Despite my not knowing what the butter cow means, I can walk away knowing it means quite a bit to a lot of people. And maybe it doesn't need to mean anything at all. Maybe I should just let the butter cow be, and that just might be good enough.

HISTORY & CHARACTERS

St. Louis' Wealthy King of the Hobos

MARC BLANC

It doesn't take many days in St. Louis to learn that the city is constituted with the names of the rich and white, the dead and old. Nineteenth-century beer barons endure as street signs long after their draughts stopped flowing. Dogfood moguls lend their names to entire college campuses, and it's impossible to forget that the major institutes of art and culture are brought to you by a handful of banking dynasties. Busch, Danforth, and Kemper might sound familiar to those outside of St. Louis, but there is one ubiquitous local name that seems to be ours alone—that of the Eads family.

They are among the oldest and richest of those already old and rich St. Louis families. The patriarch, James Buchanan Eads, worked modest jobs on Mississippi River steamboats in the early nineteenth century before developing a diving bell that could plunge men into the depths of the river, where they would salvage goods lost in shipping accidents. Businesses and families alike were willing to spend big for the recovery of their possessions, resulting in a fortune for the self-educated Eads.

Eads immortalized his family name in stone and steel in 1874, when he completed the titanic Eads Bridge, forever connecting St. Louis to East St. Louis over the Mississippi. At the behest of the city government and his friends in the railroad industry, Eads constructed the bridge to ease the flow of railway commerce into the river town. With ingenuity, generous tax breaks, and the lives of over a dozen construction workers, Eads built something more than a bridge. He built a monument to his own engineering genius and to the triumph of free trade over nature's obstacles. *A most American mythology.*

However, a counter-mythology hides in the shadow of the Eads Bridge. While most St. Louisans know James Buchanan Eads, his grandson James Eads How is consigned to the margins of even local history, where if he is remembered at all it is as an eccentric curiosity. In 1898, the younger James attained celebrity for spurning his inheritance to the family fortune and living as a shabbily dressed itinerant worker. After the death of James's father that year, a nationally circulated article announced that "the millionaire grandson of James B. Eads has given up luxuries and a palace in St. Louis for plain living and missionary work in the slums of the city." The press faithfully reported on the young man's charitable acts for the next ten years, when newspapers began to call him the "millionaire tramp." James spent his adult life riding the rails, looking for temporary manual labor and dipping into his funds only to finance his mutual aid society, the International Brotherhood Welfare Association (IBWA).

Initially, the IBWA was known for the "Hobo Colleges" that it established across the Midwest, with active operations in St. Louis, Chicago, and Cincinnati. A Harvard man, James organized and sometimes taught classes on law, public speaking, and history to the train-hoppers who happened to be in town en route to their next job. Asked why he spent his time teaching wandering laborers when he could have been lavishing in luxury, James would repeat what he had allegedly said to the mayor of St. Louis when he requested that all $20,000 of the inheritance from his father go to the city's poor instead— "Whose money is this? I didn't do anything for this." James decided that his family fortune rightfully belonged to members of America's most precarious workforce, the temporarily employed and constantly traveling class known then as "hoboes."

James Eads How around 1918.

While no historian has concluded why James felt that this particular population possessed the best claim to his millions, his decision makes a certain sense considering his family's businesses. James' father, James Flintham How, was an executive of the Wabash Railroad, one of the most succesful railways in the nineteenth- and twentieth-century Midwest. Wabash connected Ohio to Kansas City, stretching north to Michigan's Upper Peninsula. It's likely that from an early age James heard about an underclass of men who illegally stowed away on the company cars, denying his father's side of the family their train fares and his mother's side their bridge tolls.

Railroads deployed police as well as public sentiment to vilify migrant workers and prevent them from taking money out of the company pocket. James undid quite a bit of Wabash's efforts in 1915 when his mother died, leaving him in possession of his full inheritance. The tramp king immediately put his money toward what would become his seldom-cited contribution to radical American literature, a monthly magazine called the *Hobo News*.

Printed first in St. Louis and later in Cincinnati, the *Hobo News* is an unusual artifact in the history of American radical publishing. Although kept afloat by an obscenely rich man, the magazine honored the voices of the dispossessed for whom it claimed to speak. While James contributed an editorial to each issue, the masthead included several self-identified hoboes who produced the bulk of the paper's original writing.

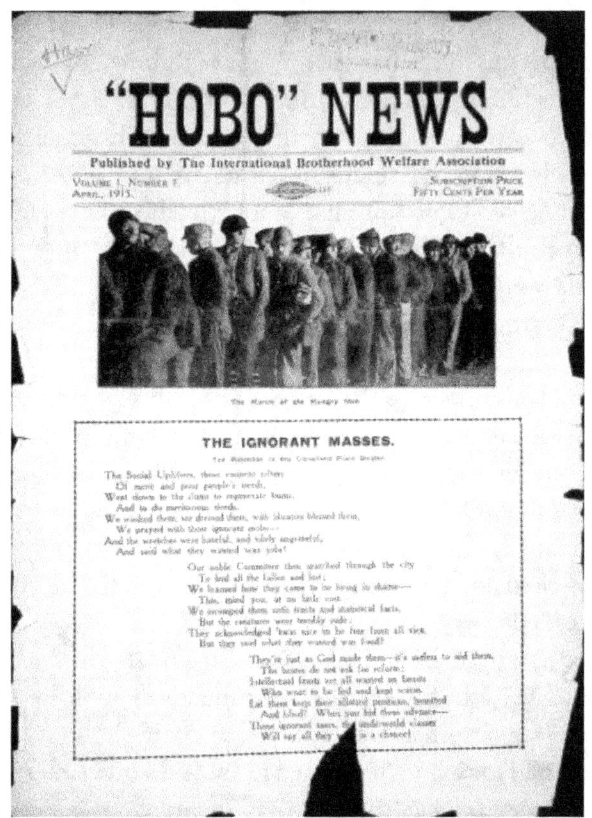

Inaugural issue of Hobo News, April 1915.

The paper's reportage consisted mainly of first-person accounts of working life on the road. In a 1918 article, Will J. Quirke, a regular contributor, recalls his experience as a prisoner of a chain gang. Quirke writes that he train-hopped to Jacksonville, Florida in response to an advertisement promising high wages for "mechanics and laborers of all kinds," only to find that the advertisement was a rouse for luring and imprisoning migrants to extort fines from them under an anti-vagrancy law. Quirke describes the horrifying violence inflicted on him and his fellow workers in custody. "For the least offense, the prisoners were stripped, laid across a barrel … I saw a big negro get fifty lashes for sassing a guard—the flesh pulled off his back—blood and skin adhering to the strap."

For Quirke's contemporary readers, the story offers a practical warning to be wary of advertisements promising work in the South unless one owns "a bank account, a good suit, a mileage book and a tin can badge with the inscription 'Special Detective.'" For readers in 2023, Quirke's article offers a window into a misrepresented subculture. Over a century's worth of popular culture has portrayed hoboes as almost invariably white and never as the victims of overt state violence. Yet Quirke witnessed Black itinerant workers who were subjected to the atrocities of slavery in the legalized form of chain gangs and anti-vagrancy laws. Over its fifteen-year run, *Hobo News* presented numerous similar scenes of working-class life from the perspectives of some of those who lived it the hardest, accounts that challenge modern assumptions about the hobo experience.

Portrait of Bill Quirke, 1918.

James Eads How exercised the lightest of editorial hands, evidenced by the non-standardized "hobo vernacular" that writers such as Quirke freely employed. Quirke illustrates one injustice of the chain gangs with heavy slang: "If a gink gets arrested and sentenced to time in the Cally if he has a few dollars or a good Benny, they give him every opportunity to get away from the working gang, so they can appropriate his money or clothes" [Translation: If a hobo with some money and decent clothing is arrested and works on a chain gang, the officers will steal his cash and sell his clothes].

Hobo News' use of this class-based dialect is as fundamental to its radicalism as the content of its journalism. The magazine's motto, "by the hoboes, for the hoboes, of the hoboes," declares James' intention to cultivate a distinct class consciousness among migratory workers. An effort focused specifically on hoboes was necessary because other centers of working-class power did not often welcome the migrant class into the organized labor movement. Outright hostility was more common than gestures of solidarity, even from radical leftists. For example, during the St. Louis General Strike of 1877, one member of the socialist Workingmen's Party publicly denounced the "tramps and vagrants" to whom mainstream newspapers libelously compared the striking railroad workers.

Against this vitriol, James claimed that his magazine's primary ambition was to "make the word 'hobo' respectable." To accomplish this, he and his staff used hobo slang, as well as ribald, absurd, and sometimes twisted humor. One headline announces "Beer-Crazed Mule Commits Suicide." Such articles appeared alongside earnest appeals to the more respected sections of the working class. In an editorial from the second issue, James tries to persuade labor leaders to pay more attention to their migrant brethren if only because underemployment caused migrants to cross the picket line during strikes. "No Union man, no matter how skillful his craft or how good his wages, can consider himself and his family safe while such conditions exist. The strike-breakers are all taken from this class [of migrant workers]." James's voice in the *Hobo News* mediates the relationship between hoboes and the marginally more privileged workers who were also reading the magazine. Drawing on his education at Harvard and Meadville Theological Seminary, he does not write in hobo dialect, opting instead for an "enlightened" Christian rhetoric inspired by the social gospel. He announces that the magazine is "against Commercialism, Unemployment and War and in favor of Co-operation, Brotherhood and Peace."

*The January 1918 cover depicts migrant workers beneath the St. Louis b
ridge engineered by James Eads How's famous father, with a somewhat
ironic "Happy New Year" greeting.*

James's ability to build a rhetorical bridge between the hoboes and
more steadily employed readers worked in the *Hobo News'* favor, if the
magazine's circulation is a reliable measure. The magazine was certainly
the most widely distributed publication of its kind, peaking at 20,000
copies per issue in 1919. Still, James was not without his critics. The
editor exacerbated a rivalry with the International Workers of the World
(Wobblies) in the pages of the *Hobo News*, critiquing the Wobblies'
militancy and questioning their compassion for itinerant labor. The
Wobblies, according to the historian John Lennon in his book *Boxcar
Politics*, saw James as "an eccentric millionaire who had no authentic
connection to the work."

The Wobblies had some ground to stand on in their criticism. James' attitude toward hoboes was not always as fraternal as it was patronizing. "We've got to organize these men," he once told a reporter. "But first we've got to educate them. Most of them have minds like children, and they don't know what organization means."

He premised his work on the belief that hoboes did not truly wish to live as hoboes. Rather, he claimed, they were victims of a volatile and unjust economic order that could not provide steady employment, a systemic failure that tempted hoboes to sinful habits like gambling and overdrinking. James believed that he had to educate them and lift them out of their degraded status, just as urgently as he had to educate polite society about their struggle. However, as Lennon argues, not all hoboes traveled because they couldn't find work. Many actively chose to live on the rails because it freed them from the managed regimentation of industrial labor. Two former hoboes, Jack London and his boxcar mentor "A-No. 1," fit this category of willing migrant. "The greatest charm of tramp-life," London waxes in his 1907 hobo memoir, *The Road*, "is the absence of monotony." Holding down the rails was, for London, "an ever changing phantasmagoria, where the impossible happens and the unexpected jumps out of the bushes at every turn." While presenting its own challenges, itinerancy offered liberty, community, and a more organic rhythm of work than the grueling factory shifts most urban Americans endured by the early twentieth century.

What cannot be said of James, however, is that he didn't live out his principles. He honored his vow of peripatetic poverty until he died in 1930, perishing from pneumonia exacerbated by severe malnutrition. James' life was a social revolution concentrated in a single individual. His work was a direct rejection of the gospel of wealth with which he was raised, and he believed in the inevitability of a freer and more just society, if only enough people would struggle for it. Maybe this is why the Eads family papers only include a handful of impersonal documents mentioning James. James Buchanan Eads impacted his world with commerce and steel; James Eads How did the same with paper and charity. Paper may perish much faster than steel, but personal immortality was never James' goal.

The gradual, complete eradication of inequality, on the other hand, was his goal. In its small way, the *Hobo News* made strides toward even this immense dream. James blurred the distinctions between consumer, sales agent, and stakeholder by encouraging readers to sell their copies of the magazine in the "Jungles" and "Hobohemias" through which they passed. Not only did this distribution model allow the magazine to quickly spread across the country, but it challenged the burgeoning hegemony of copyright law and corporatization in American publishing. The "hustlers" of the *Hobo News* differed from other sales agents because they did not have to split their earnings with James or any of the magazine's executive committee. Neither did the magazine show any qualms with reprinting articles from larger publications without attribution—most reprints were articles by sympathetic authors such as Jack London and Ambrose Bierce, unlikely to object to a socialistic hobo paper making use of their radical words. The *Hobo News* must therefore be one of the only twentieth-century publications that was simultaneously the product of a single millionaire and a collectivist, anti-profit enterprise of the dispossessed.

Members of the International Brotherhood Welfare Society, who also likely sold the Hobo News as they traveled across the country looking for work.

The dialect of the *Hobo News* has yellowed like the paper on which it was printed—although if you want to brush up on "Hoboese," the October 1919 issue features a glossary of common hobo slang. The reality of migrant labor in this country, however, is just palpable now as it was in the 1910s. Up to three million people in the U.S. leave their homes to find work every year. Most twenty-first-century migrants in the States are Latino and do not resemble James' hoboes in physical appearance or cultural practice, but current labor organizers can still learn much from James' compassion for a forgotten proletariat. Unions must attend to the needs of these populations, and their vernacular, humor, and communities ought to be recorded. But do we have—do we need—a James Eads How?

Author's Note: All imagery and quotations from *Hobo News* issues were made possible by the St. Louis Public Library, which has digitized 40 issues from the magazine's first five years of operation.

The Queer Witches of Appalachia

EMMA CIESLIK

Stephanie Starr Long, a practicing solitary witch of Melungeon descent, wakes up before 3 am every morning. In the quiet moonlight, she methodically fixes her favorite morning tea, lights honeysuckle incense, and says a prayer to her patron deity Bastet. "Thank you, Beloved daughter of Ra, for the blessings you bestow on all of us everyday." She puts on her tourmaline and obsidian bracelet to protect against negative energy, which she cleanses every night, and loads a new bag of dried cat food into her car to feed any strays she meets along her way to and from work. Feeding these animals is an act of gratitude to Bastet, an Egyptian goddess of protection and good health with the head of a cat.

When she gets home, she lights more incense and lays a small object collected during the day—for example a feather or rock—on her altar as an offering. As she cooks dinner, she sometimes uses food coloring pens to write intentions on her ingredients, such as bay leaves, recalling kitchen witchcraft common among Appalachian folk magic practitioners. After cleaning up, she writes in her journal or Book of Shadows, which she hopes to pass onto her children one day, and jumps into the tub. Sometimes she adds herbs and flowers to the bath water while sending out positive intentions for tomorrow. She ends the day by thanking Bastet again for protecting her, her house, and her family.

Long's story could take place anywhere in the United States— goddess worship is experiencing a revival along with eclectic witchcraft and paganism across the Americas and western Europe. But her rituals are closely tied to the Appalachian Mountains that she calls home, just like countless other Appalachian folk magic practitioners and witches who cast and create with the flora and fauna around them. In particular, queer Appalachians like Long, are finding spiritual homes within these traditions and among circles, covens, and support groups all along the Appalachian Trail. This is the story of the queer witches of Appalachia.

The Witches' Church

Born in Hancock County, in the town of Sneedville right on the Tennessee state line, Long was raised in the Southern Missionary Baptist Church like everyone else she knew growing up. This included her mamaw, who Long believes was a granny witch. While she knows that her grandmother would have whipped her silly for calling her such, Long remembers watching her mamaw talk fire from a burn, cure cradle cap, and use home remedies to heal ear arches. Home doctoring was and is common among isolated parts of the mountains, where granny witches incorporate spell work and ritual healing into their existing Christian beliefs and worship.

Today, a number of Appalachian folk magic practitioners still identify as Christian, or as Christian witches, to recognize their religious and cultural roots and also to avoid stigma in deeply Christian communities. In researching queer covens and folk magic circles, many people noted how church is a metaphor for spiritual meaning and community they find in their craft.

Some of Long's fondest memories with her grandmother involved hunting for mushrooms and roots together in the woods. Ever since she turned 17 and moved to middle Tennessee, she continued her grandmother's tradition and began practicing witchcraft. Long never felt comfortable in a Christian church, partially because she is bisexual and Baptist churches have long histories of psychological and physical harm and violence against LGBTQ+ individuals. But in her hometown, "it didn't really matter what church you belonged to as long as you belonged to some church." In isolated mountain communities, churches provided local support networks and hosted community discussions, often a space denied to LGBTQ+ folks.

Long was not alone. Jake "Dr. Buck" Richards, author of *Appalachian Folk Healing: A collection of Old-Time Remedies, Charms, and Spells* and *Backwoods Witchcraft: Conjure & Folk Magic from Appalachia*, also felt the pressure to be part of his family's church. Born and raised in upper East Tennessee, none of his family identified as a witch aside from his Papaw Oscar who was a water witch. His family has been rooted to the land for at least 300 years. Although his papaw was a Freewill Baptist preacher at his church and he never targeted LGBTQ+ folks on the pulpit, Richards vividly remembers guest preachers spreading hate speech. "The God spoken of at home," Richards admits, "was a different character altogether." But those experiences in church were traumatic, and up until he came out at 13, he had spent years trying to strengthen his Christian faith to make himself better.

He shared his identity after scriptural research, finding that his tears and prayers were spent trying to model his relationship with Jesus to mimic that of everyone else's that he saw, just like Long. Witchcraft provided a space for him that he felt did not exist in the world, cementing his practice in the people, objects, and nature surrounding him.

"The church had little me thinking God was out there and up there. Distant. So distant it felt like you had to take a number and wait. But I learned, through folk magic and my ancestors, that He is with me, in every action, every breath, everywhere. It also led me to learn more about Christ than the church would have ever taught me. Likewise, my work has incidentally led people back to the God of their ancestors. That wasn't my plan. I just wanted to lead them back to the magic of their home. And it turns out they made it back to a home they also felt excluded from, straight or queer."

It was in witchcraft that he found a magical queer church through which he found a community, with both his ancestors and other witches, that welcomed all of him.

Long found her own version of queer church in the Appalachian Mountains—the Pagans of Warren County—where her identity is celebrated and affirmed. "I'm not sure that being bi actually affects my path," she explained, "but my path makes being bi easier in ways.

There's no condemnation from fellow witches. There's no religious 'rules' that state I'm going to hell. There's a freedom in witchcraft to be your authentic self no matter race, creed, or sexuality." Despite leaving the Christian Church, she feels her ancestors' hands on her shoulders as she practices a uniquely Appalachian and queer witchcraft. As she firmly believes, they are proud of the woman that she has become and the knowledge she will pass onto her children.

Similarly, bisexual witch, mother, and librarian Annie Colson finds a feeling of church in the flora and fauna of the Appalachian Mountains. Although born with Appalachian blood, Colson was adopted into a family in Arizona. Raised by a Christian deacon, she discovered paganism as a form of rebellion against her parents. Soon after, she met the owners of The Astrology Store in Glendale, Arizona. The incredibly affirming and welcoming gay couple behind the counter meant the world to a young Colson, and the first person she came out to was co-owner Ray Watkins who welcomed her with open arms. She officially "came out of the broom closet" at age 16 at the same time she better understood her sexuality.

"It was in paganism," Colson elaborates, "that I first found acceptance for ALL of me, not just the parts that were easy to love, and in the community, I run, that's something that I cherish, and it's a way to keep Ray's memory alive." As an adult, Colson moved back to McMinnville, Tennessee where she found a church of her own. Colson spends her weekends barefoot in her fenced garden, where she grows corn, melons, and summer squash. She plants an abundance believing it her job to provide stewardship to the planet she calls home, and the Earth she calls church. She intentionally leaves space at the bottom of the fence for rabbits and other animals to pop through and help themselves, regularly picks up garbage while hiking, and urges others not to litter. "The Earth is my church because it's where I feel most at peace, where my soul rests, and where I can choose to remember or forget as needed." Colson's queer church is the land that surrounds her, the Appalachian Mountains in her backyard that provided the plants for her ancestors' possible herbal remedies.

Networks of Support

In a region where almost everyone is part of a church, as Long described above, covens, circles, and support groups provide witches within isolated communities and scattered across the Mountains with spiritual homes. While many groups openly welcome witches of any gender, sexual orientation, race, or creed, they also intentionally meet in safe spaces in the community and ask members to wear name tags (including personal pronouns) at each meeting. For example, Morgana Morrigan, Head Priestess for Coven 92 in Woodstock, Georgia, shared that her circle—which includes a number of LGBTQ+ members— meets at a designated safe space. They meet in a member's salon known in the area for genderless haircuts and inclusive staff.

"I think what really affirms that we are safe," Morrigan said, "is our energy and compassion towards each person who comes to check us out. We have a great mix of all different practices, ages, sexual identities, and backgrounds. We understand we are different, but are compassionate enough to still coexist together in a beautiful way." The coven gathers once a month to host classes, craft sessions, rituals, and meet and greets. Usually around 20-30 people show up, although more people participate in the yearly Samhain and Yule Potlucks held at members' homes. This year, Coven 92 hosted two astrology classes, made their own incense, painted hex signs, and practiced wax painting, met with a dream intuitive, made and danced the maypole, and hosted several rituals for members in need.

The mission of supporting members in need closely recalls churches in Appalachian communities. For LGBTQ+ individuals, where churches recall histories of harm, trauma, and violence and are socially excluded Appalachian covens and due to queerphobia, support groups like Morrigan's, and the Pagans of Warren County step up to care for their own. The Pagans of Warren County, led by Colson over the past year, developed an outreach program to help members in times of economic and personal stress, such as surgeries, loss, and new family additions. One part of this program is a meal train. The pilot will start on September 20th and provide five days of hot meals to Colson's coadmin who is having knee placement surgery.

By creating programs that provide for their members, covens, circles, and support groups acknowledge the unique stresses and challenges of being LGBTQ+ in Appalachia despite LGBTQ+ people existing in the region for decades. In fact, LGBTQ+ individuals are stepping into leadership roles in some covens like the Witches of Moonrock Mountain in Georgia, disrupting decades long traditions of straight leaders. Lord Lucian, High Priest of the Witches, explains that he, along with half of their group, identify as gay or lesbian. His group was originally initiated by family tradition, wherein straight family members led the tradition generation after generation. Lucian is the first one in his line to be gay and head a coven.

Just like Coven 92, "someone's sexuality doesn't play into our acceptance process," Lucian notes, "neither does their gender, gender identity, age, skin color, or religious background. What we look for is sincere interest and belief." In fact, the rise of LGBTQ+ leaders in covens, circles, and support groups like Lucian and Colson speaks to growing numbers of Appalachian witches acknowledging their gender identities and sexual orientations and claiming their mountain roots as key aspects of their own practice, as key parts of what make them a witch in the first place. Lucian, Colson, and Richards also represent growing numbers of LGBTQ+ Appalachian witches leading their communities in inclusive practice and outreach.

Finding the queer witches

LGBTQ+ Appalachian witches, Long explains, are rare finds. For Long, this was mostly the result of Appalachian culture and a deeply Christian tradition keeping people in both types of closets. But as Richards explained, this does not erase the fact that queer people have existed in Appalachia for centuries, and in queer witches. "Love has always been fighting in these mountains." The forces that kept and keeps people from coming out as LGBTQ+ and from practicing their witchcraft and folk magic freely and openly make finding community difficult, as Long found out, but new social media platforms like Facebook are connecting folks in isolated mountainous regions across the Eastern United States and raising awareness about existing groups in the region, such as Coven 92 and the Pagans of Warren County.

When asked about how this research will increase representation, she explained: "what I would like people to know is simple. We exist! We are out here. We have NOT given up our love of our mountain upbringing, we have not given up our traditions and our culture just because we are witches or LGBTQ! We are proud Appalachians; we are proud witches. We've always been here, we'll always be here, and we'll continue to pass down our knowledge and our love of the mountains, our love of folk magic, to the next generation to come." Beyond new digital platforms,

Colson, Lucian, and Richards roles as leaders in the Appalachian witch community increase representation of queer Appalachian witches and inspire others to join groups.

For example, I met Camille Rivera, a queer witch whose family has lived in the Kentucky Appalachian Mountains for generations, through the Appalachian Traditional Witches: Hedge Witches, Old Craft, Folk Magic Facebook group. Rivera explained the importance of openly identifying as Appalachian as well as LGBTQ+, fighting histories of classicism inside the witch community and the region and destabilizing Appalachia as a stereotypically straight place.

Rivera was born and raised in the Appalachian region, as were her parents, and their parents before them. Her mother is from Lewis County, Kentucky, and her dad is from Carter County, Kentucky, met and married in Rowan County where Rivera was raised. Like other Appalachian families, the terms "witch" and "witchcraft" were taboo and her family went to the non-denominational Wallingford Community Church in Kentucky. Inside the church, many people practiced folk magic, including her grandmother who used local plants in herbal healing and was clairvoyant and her mother who inherited the same abilities. As discussed frequently in the family, her grandmother used a tea mixture to cure her mother's scarlet fever, and Rivera's own mother healed her colic with catnip tea.

Her mother's clairvoyance was also striking, receiving premonitions as clear as day, and while Rivera has experienced several, she believes her abilities will develop further with time. All of her family members who possess the ability in her family lose their sight as this power develops, she explained. She is grateful that her family was supportive when she came out three years ago, offering nothing but love and understanding. She is also not the only queer Appalachian witch, she counts one of her cousins as well, and while she currently lives in Columbus, Ohio for work, she plans to move back to Martinsville, Virginia where her mom lives to be back in the Appalachian Mountains.

In her experiences, coming out as LGBTQ+ and coming out of the broom closet went hand in hand for her. "I think that once you've broken that barrier of being LGBTQ and you've acknowledged that there's something different about you in a rural area where some people can be really resistant to anything different, it's not that much harder to openly acknowledge your witchcraft and to not be afraid to call it what it is." Just like Long, Rivera explained that being an LGBTQ+ Appalachian witch is about being true to herself and her ancestors, acknowledging and upholding practices that have been passed down through her family for generations. This is a slow and steady movement as people find the courage to acknowledge their multifaceted identities and how they coexist with their Appalachian heritage.

"I think, in a way, a lot of us are conditioned to be ashamed of being a 'hillbilly.'" Rivera said. "Whether by outsiders or by our own families, I think some of us develop internalized shame and stigma around being poor, having an accent, coming from a rural area with not a lot of access to important healthcare and so on. I think it's a positive thing that more and more people are openly embracing themselves and shedding the shame." To be a queer Appalachian witch is to dismantle the classist, sexist, and religious systems of oppression that exist locally and nationally, as well as classicism that exists within the witchcraft community itself. To be a queer Appalachian is to challenge family and group gatekeeping of magical knowledge.

Witchcraft has for centuries been a spiritual refuge for LGBTQ+ abandoned, oppressed, and harmed by Christian churches, especially in Appalachian regions, and with more LGBTQ+ Appalachian people taking on leadership roles, the queer part of Appalachian folk magic is becoming more apparent and celebrated. In doing so, the queer Appalachian witches of today are sustaining their legacies by making their covens, circles, and support groups welcoming environments for the next generation. As Richards poetically said, "Just as in everything else, every queer Appalachian person is an answered prayer of one of their ancestors."

All photographs are courtesy of Lord Lucian, a queer high priest of the Witches of Moonrock Mountain, and depict their Mabon celebration on Saturday, September 23, 2023.

This article is dedicated to all LGBTQ+ witches around the United States who are persecuted, abused, or killed because of their identities, including Colson's mentor Ray Watkins who was killed outside his shop in 2020.

Hatchet-Throwing in Forgotten Places

HANNAH KENNEDY

Each summer when I was growing up in Oil City, Pennsylvania, my siblings and I looked forward to Youth Field Day in July, when kids from the community would spend a whole Saturday in the woods, learning the skills of outdoorsmanship. The event was led by the local chapter of the Izaak Walton league, helmed by grandfatherly mountain men who were tasked with passing on our Northern Appalachian traditions of resilience and self-sufficiency. The kids were joined by their parents and grandparents (in our case, Dad and Grandpa), with the goal being to take part in these activities as a family.

Our summer field days went like this - we got up early and piled into Grandpa's green pickup truck, driving a few miles out of town down Deep Hollow Road, which carves up the space between two steep hillsides. We turned off onto a gravel driveway which wound its way through the forest, on stone bridges over the creek, and finally to a large rough clearing surrounded by thick tree cover. We joined the dozens of other kids at the main building, where we signed in, got free tee-shirts (a different color each year) and grabbed a quick breakfast of fruit and pop-tarts.

Then, the games began. The Izaak Walton grounds, officially called Waltonian Park, covered about sixty acres of land and a few buildings. A large pond sat in the middle of the grounds, as did an ancient water fountain and rusting swings and slides, and a weird stone memorial fenced off and a little overgrown. A few hundred yards away, a gun range extended down into a small valley, and trails probed into the thick forest like tendrils of a vine. It was all very rustic for sure. The main building and various pavilions had only the bare necessities and were decorated with a generous collection of taxidermied animals. The head of an albino deer mounted on one wall always seemed to bore into my soul with its eerie red eyes.

The day was broken into short increments, and each child was organized into a team based on age group. Then, each group rotated through different activities. So every field day, we had a chance to do everything - archery; fishing lure-making; target shooting with a .22, target shooting with a shotgun, and target shooting with a muzzleloader; an obstacle course; hatchet-throwing (which I was terrible at, and definitely responsible for my team losing for); canoeing on the pond, fishing on the pond (taking care to avoid the black snakes nestled in the sunny grass); interactive sessions on identifying animals and plants; and trapping (have you ever seen a bear trap up close? My tibia bones shudder even thinking about it).

While I haven't pursued the majority of these activities in adulthood, I appreciate that this kind of event existed - an educational, interactive, fun environment for kids to learn about the outdoors, the kinds of skills one needs to survive in a rural community. This experience instilled in me a value I still hold to this day: that education is the single most powerful way to understand how the world works, to preserve a way of life, to protect from potential dangers, and to empower people for whatever comes next.

Of course, I didn't really think about all of that as a kid. I just liked making a pretty, hot-pink fishing lure, and showing the teenage archery instructor that despite his protestations to the contrary, it *is,* in fact, possible to shoot a right-handed bow with one's left hand.

It wasn't until later, as I pursued a career in writing and discovered my deep love for the forgotten post-industrial places of my homeland, that I learned the whole context about this place. I learned that Waltonian Park was not always Waltonian Park. It was not always a remote backwoods outpost with a shooting range. Instead, it was one of the largest attractions in the surrounding region, bringing families, thrill-seekers, and parties from miles around.

This place was Monarch Park, an enormous amusement park in what is now the middle of the woods.

From the 1890s to the 1920s, Monarch Park operated in full swing. Featuring a merry-go-round, dance hall, bowling alleys, botanical gardens, waterfall, a Ferris wheel and rollercoaster, shopping, picnic facilities, fine dining, *and more,* the park saw up to 15,000 visitors on summer weekends, a number which grew up to 30,000 on holiday weekends. Situated in Venango County, Pennsylvania between the towns of Oil City and Franklin, it was just a trolley ride away for hours of fun.

At the time, this region, the Oil Region, was still the center of the oil industry. And while the frenzy of the oil boomtowns had mostly mellowed, Venango County, PA was still the place to be. And up until the end of the Roaring 20s, so was Monarch Park.

Parties of thousands gathered in the restaurant and picnic pavilion for private parties and holidays. People enjoyed dancing in the two-story dance hall, listening to music from the outdoor orchestra pit, riding on the miniature train, drinking from the natural spring fountains, idling on the playground swings and slides, testing their strength and endurance in organized races and contests, and of course, enjoying the typical amusement park diversions of Ferris wheel, carousel, and roller-coaster. At the center of the park, a 120-foot tower featuring elegant glass windows and a domed roof dazzled with electric light. The park held celebrations for holidays like Memorial Day and the Fourth of July, culminating in marvelous fireworks shows.

By the end of World War I and the onset of the 1920s, however, the popularity of the park tapered off. The 1920s brought an even greater popularity of that American mainstay: the car. People began travelling farther for vacations and holidays. By the end of the 1920s, Monarch Park folded, and the facility was sold to a few buyers before coming into the possession of the Izaak Walton League. Even though various plans were proposed to keep at least some of the attractions going, none came to fruition, and the park structures sat abandoned and derelict until eventually they were torn down or destroyed by the elements. Some buildings were dismantled, and the materials used for other projects in the community. In fact, the floorboards of the two-story dance hall were used to build three houses in the neighborhood I grew up in.

There's something that hits me when I think about all of this: when I compare maps of the old park layout to the modern satellite images of rugged forests and creeks; especially when I consider the many extant pictures of a hundred smiling faces gathered around the playgrounds or picnic pavilion, of couples dancing in their elegant party clothes, of the band members shyly mugging the camera between sets. To the people in these photos, captured in a moment of light and movement and fun, the place they were in must have seemed so permanent, so fixed in the grand scheme of life.

What really hits me is the sheer amount of time I spent in this place—hours over entire days, over several years—with no idea of what it was. The pond I canoed and fished in is where the carousel used to be. The main building where I ate strawberry pop-tarts, while staring at the creepy taxidermized albino deer on the wall, was the site of the original picnic pavilion. I showed my prowess for archery on the old picnic grounds. I shot .22 rifles next to the site of the two-story restaurant, and shotguns near the bandstand. I learned about bear traps next to the rollercoaster. I played on those rusted swings, left over from a century before. And the weird stone memorial that was fenced off and overgrown? It was the foundation of the 120-foot Electric Tower.

It's no surprise that from a young age I was familiar with the experience of being in a place and sensing its long-forgotten history all around me: the Oil Region (and the Rust Belt as a whole) are rife with places that no longer bear resemblance to what they used to be. It is a fact often lamented.

But even before I knew this place as Monarch Park, something about the scattered foundations, the random metal tracks half-buried in the earth, and the elegant stone bridges over the creek, clued me in to something greater going on. It was as if the memory of the place, the memories of all the people who had spent their many hours there just as I was, were quietly whispering to me, begging me to take another look.

I get sentimental about places, especially forgotten ones like Monarch Park. They're a bit of a bummer, a bit sobering, a bit sad. But I think it's a good kind of sadness. It's the kind of sadness that reminds us that life is short: our joy and sorrow are fleeting, the places and people we love are temporary and the extent to which the world will remember us is limited. We don't like to think about this as human beings. We like to think we're the main characters of the world's story, the center of it all, like a 120-foot Electric Tower of light rising high above a magnificent amusement park.

In reality, we are not permanent fixtures in the world. Instead, we are... people. Spending a little time here before moving on, experiencing great joy and pain and doing our best to create beautiful moments wherever we can. Like the many forgotten people in these pictures, our story is short, but the joy and beauty left in our wake are not insignificant. When I look at the faces in these pictures, I see a moment of life, which is in itself a thing of value.

I see a place that was beloved, and I am inspired to bestow all forgotten places with that honor again.

The Ax Man Cometh, Again

NICHOLAS MAINIERI

It is the time-honored tradition of the relief pitcher to make ridiculous catches while shagging flyballs during pregame batting practice, and John Axford settles beneath a pop-up in shallow center, attempting a Mays-esque basket catch. He bricks it and the ball rolls free. He spikes his glove in the grass, gives it a kick—comedically, a show for the teammates watching and ragging.

First pitch in Team Canada's 2023 World Baseball Classic match-up with Great Britain is two hours hence, here at Chase Field in Phoenix, Arizona.

Now Axford's redemption lofts in the form of a short flare behind second. When he muffs it again he takes his glove off and punts it like a football.

As batting practice concludes, the grounds crew scurries and the Canadian ballplayers flee for the clubhouse. Ax jogs in from center to the pitcher's mound. He toes the rubber and looks in for an imaginary sign and comes set. He is six-five-and-a-half, 240 pounds or so. Gone is the feathered lettuce that once cascaded from the back of his cap, and a full, significantly gray beard has long since replaced the handlebar mustache with which he first rose to prominence, thirteen years ago, as the endearingly aesthete fireballer closing out games for the Milwaukee Brewers. Among the sleeve of tattoos on his left arm is a still frame from his favorite film, the neo-noir classic *Le Samouraï*. He wears his former Brewers number, 59, on his red Canadian jersey. He is two weeks shy of his 40th birthday.

On the hill, he relaxes his stance and looks around the stadium, taking it all in. He cranes his neck, staring up the steep flights of the grandstand. Overhead, the retractable roof has shuttered like some otherworldly exoskeleton of giant steel plates and arching ribs. Commerce flashes in the hangared air, the jumbotron and banner LEDs, neon advertisements, cold beer. Beneath it all is the well-tended garden, the green Bermuda grass, the red-brown clay, the sharp white foul lines and equidistant bases. Old patterns softly abide an ever-glitzier world.

And this, gathering the view from the mound before the game, is a habit Ax developed during his rookie year in Milwaukee. There's so much going on in a Major League stadium, and you don't want the moment you've been called upon, in a tough late-game situation, to be the first time you've encountered it all. After he's come off the field, Ax chuckles. "And it's been a long time since I pitched in this ballpark."

(It's been eight years, in fact. He closed out a 6-4 victory for the Rockies against the Diamondbacks on July 5, 2015, striking out Paul Goldschmidt with the tying runs aboard.)

"I saw those basket catches out there," I say.

"I clanked all of them!" he cries, and shows me his glove, a brand new and still inflexible Rawlings. He'd needed a new glove for the tournament—his old one had gotten too beat up over the last year while he coached his son's youth baseball team—but he'd not had time to break it in properly. He muses, "I better use two hands if I have to cover first today."

I am moderately terrified for him but try not to show it.

"I'm gonna go hydrate and get some of these nerves out. I think I'm in there today."

And here's exactly the thing. John Axford has pitched in 544 Major League games, but only *one* in the last five years. He massages the scar on his elbow and descends into the dugout.

The end of things—for all but the rare superstars who take retirement victory laps—is typically sudden or unexpected and almost always unceremonious, if not outright tragic. Time, I suppose, is undefeated. Smarter people than me have called baseball itself an antidote to that plain fact, but I'm not sure how you square it with the other oft-cited observation that baseball is best understood as a game designed to break your heart.

Ax and I have known each other since college, when we were teammates at the University of Notre Dame, more than half our lifetimes ago. Music is a defining social factor in baseball clubhouses the world over, and I remember well the encyclopedically eclectic mixes when he had command of the clubhouse stereo. The B-52s' "Rock Lobster" was in frequent rotation one year. We connected, in part, because we both favored harder genres. We each also trafficked in the creative arts. Ax majored in film production and critical studies, and I watched a number of movies for the first time on his recommendation—the Korean mindbender *Oldboy*, for instance. Years later, in 2017, I'd written a novel and happened to be visiting a Toronto-area bookstore for an event. Three people showed—John Axford and his two children, J.B. and Jameson.

We caught up on Zoom in early March, about a week before the World Baseball Classic. Ax was sitting in his home, in Burlington, Ontario, in front of a series of his photographs hanging on the wall. Each was the same shot, the western view from his place in Oakland, when he'd pitched for the A's—the foregrounded bay, the distant San Francisco skyline, the vast, vertically arranged sky. But each had been taken at a different time, under different conditions, and the diminutive skyline floated in a spectrum of blue, orange, red, gray. Ghosts in sheets of fog. Each on its own was a fine photo, but together they struck me as a statement on patience, an argument for empathy and subtlety, how detail reveals itself to the dedicated, open mind.

"Oh," Ax interrupted himself, hefting his iPad toward something, "can you hear that?"

Coyotes were howling in his backyard.

In March of 2020, he'd been a free agent preparing for Canada's Olympic qualifiers when the pandemic put a stop to everything. He'd finally gotten healthy after two rough years—a broken leg with the Dodgers in 2018, and a Blue Jays' campaign in 2019 that never began due to an injury in Spring Training and subsequent bone spur—but, with COVID lockdowns, he spent 2020 at home with J.B. and Jameson. He entertained himself by becoming a close study of the coyotes around his home, setting up his cameras by the window and observing them daily.

"I like to think they're my buddies now," he told me over Zoom.

It is not a coincidence that the uniquely pressured work environment of the baseball closer has tended to suit some of the modern game's most idiosyncratic personalities. The famous axiom about the best players failing most of the time does not extend to this guy—it is the opposite, in fact, and at the extreme end of the spectrum—so neither is it coincidence that the role provides, arguably, the game's most volatile career path. Late-inning relievers have been commonplace strategy for half a century, but only eight of 272 ballplayers enshrined in Cooperstown are relief pitchers. The Mariano Riveras and Trevor Hoffmans are few and far between. As a current MLB closer told me, in Arizona, "Relievers have to prove themselves time and again. People are always telling you that you can't do it anymore."

As the jobless pandemic wore on for Ax, he joined the Canadian network *Sportsnet* to contribute on-camera pitching commentary. By the summer of 2021 he hadn't pitched in a Big League ballgame in nearly three years, but the Olympic qualifiers were back on so he laced up his spikes for his country. When he was suddenly blowing lively 98-mph fastballs past professional hitters again, the Blue Jays offered him a minor league deal, signing him right out of their own network's television studio. He was 38 years old.

He spent July of 2021 with Toronto's Triple-A farm team in Buffalo, NY, throwing as well as he ever had. He averaged 97-98 mph on his fastball, and in a month's work he posted an 0.84 ERA and relinquished a grand total of two base hits, the second being a broken bat infield dribbler in his final minor league outing.

Another organization had called with the intent to bring him to the Big Leagues.

The Milwaukee Brewers.

Ax originally made his MLB debut in 2009 as a September call-up with the Brewers. He began the following year in Triple-A Nashville, and I saw him that spring when his team had come down to New Orleans, where I was living at the time. After a game, we met up for burgers and drinks at Port of Call on the edge of the French Quarter and then we walked Frenchmen St., go-cups in-hand. A brass band was playing on the corner. Music spilled out from the small clubs. Ax was sporting a ridiculous/excellent handlebar mustache but thought he'd alter the look soon. A few days later, however, Milwaukee called him up for good. The Milwaukee faithful loved the stylized lip sweater and its echoes of Brewers' legend Rollie Fingers, so it stayed.

The media loved him, too. "Colorful, open—I enjoyed him a lot," Ken Rosenthal told me of the times he engaged with Ax. "He made it fun, which is not always true." The John Axford origin story was told repeatedly on broadcasts and in newspapers—how he'd begun 2009 as a bartender at an East Side Mario's restaurant near his home in Canada, and how, the year before that, he'd been out of baseball entirely, hawking cell phones at the mall when he set up a pseudo-tryout that drew only a single regional scout, Jay Lapp of the Brewers.

Before all of that, he'd been a pro-prospect in high school and college. I was there at practice in the fall of 2003, the beginning of Ax's draft-eligible junior year, when he struck out a batter to end an intersquad inning and felt a sharp zing down his forearm. We tried to greet him with high fives at the foul line, but he answered us in a kind of vacant voice, "I think I just blew out my elbow." He had Tommy John surgery soon thereafter, and surgeons rebuilt his ulnar collateral ligament with a part of his hamstring. The following summer I was often his rehab catch partner. Ax was lankier back then, something stork-like in the look of his skinny frame, and watching him learn how to throw all over again was like seeing a six-five baby bird trying to fly. His rehab was a slow one, and after he graduated from Notre Dame, he transferred to Canisius College to pursue a master's degree and play his final year of collegiate eligibility.

All that's to say the comeback is kind of a hallmark of John Axford's pitching career.

———————————

Ax became the Brewers' closer in 2010, replacing his friend and mentor, Hall-of-Famer Trevor Hoffman (there's a delightful anecdote about Hoffman buying Ax, a rookie, his first ever complete suit when he'd needed one for the Big League airplanes). Before long, fake mustaches and foam axes were general among the Miller Park crowd, and the stadium rocked whenever his walkout music, the suitably eclectic "New Noise" by punk avant-gardists Refused, began to play. (And lest you think he came to this by inauthentic means, he owns the band's 1998 album, *The Shape of Punk to Come: A Chimerical Bombination in 12 Bursts*, on vinyl).

The following year, 2011, Ax set franchise records and led the league with 46 saves, which included a streak of 43 consecutive en route to Milwaukee winning the Central Division championship. He finished among the top ten vote-getters for the Cy Young Award and was named National League reliever of the year (an award then sponsored by Rolaids).

During the season, Jonathan Jackson—CEO of the nonprofit organization Milwaukee Film—learned through the Brewers Community Foundation that the team's star closer had studied film and loved the arts. Nowadays, the Milwaukee Film Festival is a ten-day event in the spring that draws more than 100K attendees, but in 2011 it took place in the fall, during the Brewers' postseason run. Still, Ax accepted an invitation to attend opening night of the festival and "somehow," Jackson says, "cajoled several of his teammates into attending with him."

Ax became a financial supporter of the nonprofit that next year, according to Jackson, "underwriting, specifically, our support for local filmmakers, especially student work." When I asked Ax about this, he told me he'd thought back to his own undergraduate days and how production students had had to pay out of pocket to purchase and develop their film, so he'd wanted to help with awards that would stay local to Milwaukee and those who maybe needed a little extra help to make their art, hopefully making it easier for them to bring their talents to a wider audience.

For the Brewers, however, 2012 had been a disappointing year. The team stalled at the All-Star Break, left for dead in the standings, and Ax himself was removed from the closer's role in July. In retrospect, his stat sheet is not that poor—he saved 35 games overall, good enough for sixth in the league—but in his own words, "I struggled a lot that year."

As the season wore on, however, the team started playing better and Ax was reinstated as closer in August, where he converted 17 of his final 18 save opportunities. The team went into the final weeks of the season with an outside shot at the playoffs.

The Brewers visited Cincinnati, division leaders, for their penultimate series, and there was no room for error after splitting the first two games. On getaway day, Ax entered the game in the ninth with the Brewers clinging to a 1-0 lead. He quickly struck out Zack Cozart and Joey Votto to begin the inning, but with just one out to get, Todd Frazier hit Ax's first pitch out of the ballpark to tie the game. Then Jay Bruce singled. Then Dioner Navarro hit a walk-off gapper, and the Brewers' postseason prospects evaporated.

In the somber visitors' clubhouse, Ax spoke with the media, showered, and changed. He was a professional, and today hadn't gone the way he'd wanted it to. The team got on the plane and flew back to Milwaukee. Ax got in his car at the airport and started driving home.

"As I'm on the highway, I start feeling like I'm going to lose it. And then, Yeah, it's gonna happen. I start crying and I pull over to the side of the interstate and park and put on the hazards and bawl for, like, five minutes, thinking, I fucked this up, I fucked this up for the whole team. If I'd just pitched better this year, or if I just didn't blow this last one, then we'd have a chance to get into the playoffs again after such a big year last year."

It was the culmination of an emotionally taxing year, inextricable from the broader fate of a city's baseball team. But from another vantage, this is also a prosaic if often hidden moment of deeply human overwhelm, to which pro athletes are not, of course, immune.

"Anyone can have a moment like that based on anything. Mine just happened to be because I felt like a failure for giving up a home run to Todd Frazier."

Ax wiped off the tears, put the car back in drive, and drove home.

By the trade deadline the following season, 2013, the Brewers would deal him to St. Louis, where he'd prove himself anew amid a Cardinals' World Series run. Eventually, he would pitch for six other Major League teams—Cleveland, Pittsburgh, Colorado, Oakland, Toronto, and the Los Angeles Dodgers. No matter where he was pitching, however, he kept close to Milwaukee Film and returned annually to the city in order to remain involved with the Film Festival.

One year he introduced *The Princess Bride* at the children's film series. Several other years running, *not* in the children's segment, he presented rare prints of Kubrick films, *2001* and *Dr. Strangelove,* and in 2015, when he was with the Rockies, he returned to Milwaukee to present *The Shining* on 35mm for the film's 35th anniversary. He conscripted his pal and Milwaukee barber Jess and one of her friends to dress up as the Grady girls, while he put together a spot-on Danny Torrance costume and rode an adult Big Wheel onto the stage. "That Big Wheel is still somewhere in Milwaukee," Ax says, laughing. In 2016, while with Oakland, he co-curated a sports documentary series for the festival, presenting the film *Fastball* himself. And, of course, he's sponsored and presented the entries in the *Cream City Cinema Program*, the festival's series of local films and the awards for Milwaukee's undergraduate filmmakers.

Over the years, Ax says, a lot of those young filmmakers have blossomed and gone on to keep making bigger and better things, "and I love seeing that." It's easier for artists to keep working hard, he says, when they know that others out there care, when others take an interest. "I think that's why I keep coming back to the Film Festival. I just kind of like being there for that."

But when he flew back to Milwaukee on the morning of August 2, 2021, it was due to the fact he was suddenly a Brewer again. People greeted him warmly in the hotel lobby and on the street, "properly friendly interactions." He received avalanches of text and social media messages. At the ballpark there were many familiar faces in the clubhouse and a lot of memories in the home bullpen. In truth, he was a bit overcome by it all. He considered asking Brewers manager Craig Counsell—who'd been his 2011 teammate—for a day just to process everything. "But then I was like, Nah, I'm not that guy. I'm just ready to go."

So that night the call came down to the bullpen: Ax, you've got the ninth.

One imagines what Counsell must have been thinking. The Brewers had a comfortable six-run lead over the Pirates, the perfect opportunity for the big guy to finish a game in this ballpark again. He'd done it for the Brewers 179 times before. What a cool moment this will be.

The frenetic guitar riff, the bass amassing behind it like a thunderhead—the opening notes of his old walkout music told the 23,563 in attendance all they needed to know, and it was muscle memory, nostalgia, as they rose to their feet, chopping their arms like axes. When the bullpen door opened and John Axford stepped out, the stadium erupted, the song's first lyric—*Can I scream?!*—perfectly in sync. The jumbotron flashed decade-old highlights, graphics of cartoon axes, fan-drawn signs of mustaches and slogans like the ax man cometh.

On the broadcast they exclaimed:

"The Ax Man!"

"Man, I got goosebumps!"

"John Axford, trying to finish off a game for the Brewers in *2021*."

"And bringing it still!" as his first pitch, a 95-mph sinker was fouled off by Bryan Reynolds, the Pirates' all-star centerfielder.

To Ax, however, the two-seamer had stayed flat. And while the velocity was still high, it was a few mph beneath what he'd averaged for the previous month in Triple-A. Things usually worked the other way around, a boost due to the adrenaline. A few pitches later he was more concerned—no sink to the sinker, no cut to the cutter. Yet he felt OK physically and thought he could just battle through it. On the eighth pitch of the at-bat, he started a sinker inside on Reynolds, but it stayed straight and drilled him, "which I just don't do." That's pretty much true; of 2305 batters-faced in his MLB career, he registered only 16 hit-by-pitches.

The next three Pirates ripped the ball, a lineout and two singles, loading the bases. *Oh*, Ax recalls thinking, *this is not going well.* He hadn't seen solid contact in a month, but here was one laser after another. He rationalized—these were Big League hitters again, after all—but with the next batter, pinch hitter Ben Gamel, "That's when I really started feeling it."

He missed outside, 94 mph.

He missed further out, 93 mph.

The velocity continued to fall with the next pitch, and in the video his mechanics seem more labored, as if the baseball was suddenly heavier.

The fourth ball to Gamel was way outside, and "I felt it go."

Instead of a zing down the forearm like in college, this was a shock through his triceps. He'd later find out that the reconstructed ligament in his elbow, the hamstring tendon that had been put there 18 years before, had calcified to the point where it simply broke apart.

Ax waved Counsell out with his glove. On the broadcast, you can see a quick flash of disbelief, or anguish, on the manager's face. He walked out with trainer Dave Yeager.

"It's my elbow," Ax told them. "It's not good."

When Ax walked off the mound, his eyes were downcast. Early in his career he'd noticed that when he looked into the crowd after a poor outing he'd immediately find the guy who was yelling at him. But now, walking off the field for potentially the last time in his playing career, he wanted to look, to take it all in for a moment longer. He raised his face and scanned from the outfield to the dugout. To a person, the Milwaukee fans were on their feet and applauding. Ax lowered his face again, for different reasons.

On Zoom, a week before the 2023 World Baseball Classic, Ax tried to describe this feeling for me. "I've never been able to, really, like—" He stopped and collected himself. "I've wanted to figure out, for quite a while now, how to thank the Milwaukee community and the fans within it for embracing me the way they did in that one game again."

I'd contend that his support for the city's young artists is one way he's already done so.

In Arizona, he's down there in the Canadian bullpen, sort of milling about. He's up and down, stretching, snacking, hydrating, joking with the other pitchers. The nerves are intense, how it's always been waiting for the call. It's been a lengthy, high-scoring game, ever since the British lads knocked Canada's starting pitcher, the Cleveland Guardians' Cal Quantrill, out of the game in the first. But now Canada extends their lead over Great Britain late in the game, and the call comes to the bullpen for Ax to get hot. Everything steadies for him, like it always has.

But prior to arriving in Arizona, his rehab and hopeful readiness had been touch-and-go, quite frankly. He'd taken himself through a series of ramp-ups and rest periods, but the interval between necessary rests seemed to be shrinking. He'd thrown off a mound only a few times. About two weeks ago, he'd thrown 40 pitches and tried to heat it up like a real game. *Went as well as it could,* he texted. *Haha. Arm is still attached!* He'd gotten his fastball into the upper 80s and topped out at 91, not bad for where he was in the process nor his age, but still a far cry from where he used to be (or needed to be, if he wanted to be able to get professional hitters out). He told me he thought he'd run into some physical or mental barrier, and his body simply refused any more velocity. "We'll see what happens when a hitter gets in there." Still, his elbow was angry, and he'd relied on massage therapy and dry needling to flush the inflammation. On Zoom, he chuckled and indicated his elbow, saying, "Hopefully it'll fight its last fight."

____

"Axy," Bob Uecker had said in the Brewers' clubhouse kitchen, a couple days after Ax reinjured himself against the Pirates. "People just don't fucking get it."

Uecker is one of the only people who calls him "Axy," he says, "which I love." He'd confided in Uecker that he was confused about whether he should undergo a second Tommy John (TJ) surgery. Many had told him there'd be no point. He was 38 years old, after all, and he'd made it back for that one game with the Brewers—maybe that was triumph enough? But it was hard for Ax to accept that he'd worked as hard as he had during the last few discouraging years only for his elbow to give out in a single incomplete outing.

When _I_ think of Bob Uecker I think of Harry Doyle in _Major League_ or the father in _Mr. Belvedere_ or the YouTube clips of him on Johnny Carson, so I forget that he was a Big League ballplayer before all of that, which must mean—self-deprecating humor aside—that he's got an extra competitive gear or two under the hood himself. My point is that Uecker must be naturally hilarious in the same way that people keep telling me Ax is empathetic or erudite or fun; it simply means there's a whole other level of intensity hidden beneath it all. I spoke with Mariners' catcher Tom Murphy, for instance, before Canada's exhibition against Seattle in their spring training complex. In 2015, Murphy had been a rookie catcher with the Rockies when Ax was their closer. He described Ax as a great teammate and as someone who dressed funny on the planes, "kind of artsy," who kept things loose and always had cameras with him. But when Ax came in to pitch, it was like he "flipped a switch," and his presence changed. He was intimidating. "I was just a rookie," Murphy said, "trying not to mess things up for him."

I think that's what Uecker meant when he told Ax people wouldn't understand why he wanted to get the surgery, age and prospects be damned. If the injury was the thing he had left to compete with, then that was what he was built to do.

"Yeah, that's how I feel about it," Ax remembers saying. "If I don't get the surgery, it would feel like giving up. If I do and nothing comes from it, well, at least I gave it a shot."

"Fuck yeah, Axy," Bob Uecker said. Or something like it.

Still, John was realistic. At least 2281 TJ surgeries have been performed on professional ballplayers, dating back to the very first one, on pitcher Tommy John, in 1974. This is according to data maintained by the baseball writer Jon Roegele. Six of the 2281 were players at Ax's age or older, and of those, only one, long-time closer Joe Nathan, had had the surgery for a second time. Perusing those individuals' career stats demonstrates extremely diminished professional returns, as one might expect. "In my mind," Ax says, "it was never, I'm going to have Tommy John surgery and come back and play professionally again. It was always, I'm going to do this because I'll feel like I'm giving up if I don't. Then I'll make the best of what I can with it."

He had the procedure on September 1, 2021. Surgeons took a tendon from his other hamstring this time and reconstructed his UCL. They built an internal brace around it, essentially a collagen-dipped Kevlar shoestring that they drilled into his arm bones. They put him on a conservative 18-month rehab program, standard for repeat TJ recoveries, "even though, as they told me, my original Tommy John was older than some of the people who are getting the surgery now." He looked at the calendar and saw that 18 months would put him exactly at the 2023 World Baseball Classic. Maybe that would be it, he thought. Maybe that's what I'll work toward.

In the summer of 2022, before he had even started throwing again, he attended Baseball Canada's awards banquet, celebrating the recent inductees into the Canadian Baseball Hall of Fame. At the reception he approached Ernie Whitt, the former Big Leaguer who's managed Canadian national teams for more than two decades. Ax had pitched for him before.

"Hey, just so you know," Ax told him, "all I'm going to be preparing for is the World Baseball Classic, so keep me in mind."

On the field in Arizona, Whitt was asked how it had come about, that John Axford was on the team again. "Well," Whitt quipped, "he's a lot bigger than me."

Sixteen of John Axford's family members are in the crowd at Chase Field when Ax starts his jog in from the left-field bullpen, including his three sisters and their spouses and their children. His dad, Brian, wears a #59 Brewers T-shirt. Ax's mom, Vera, scoots to the edge of her seat and recalls watching his elbow injury on television, "and I know he's a grown man but I'm still his mother and I wished I could have reached through the TV to hug him." Ax's children, J.B (11) and Jameson (10) are on their feet, cheering, waving Canadian flags. They remember their dad hobbling around the house post-surgery, since TJ recovery is also recovery from having had a part of your hamstring removed. Last summer, J.B. was his dad's first rehab catch partner.

Ax makes his warmup pitches on the mound—sinker, cutter, curveball—but the scoreboard isn't registering velocities yet. A few days ago, when he'd faced three batters in a successful exhibition outing against the Chicago Cubs, his warm-up tosses maxed out at 87-mph.

Britain's DH, Justin Wylie, steps into the box. Ax looks in as the Canadian catcher, the Guardians' Bo Naylor, flashes a sign. Ax sets and throws, a sinker for a strike.

The scoreboard registers 94 mph.

Ax attacks Wylie with a mix of sinkers and cutters and when the count is 2-2 he reaches back for a high fastball. The scoreboard flashes 95 mph.

"I saw that," Ax tells me later, laughing. "I almost retired right there."

He comes back with a curveball and gets a swing and a miss for the strikeout.

Britain's next hitter, catcher Ural Forbes, gets three straight sinkers, grounding the third between first and second base. Canada's first-baseman, Dodgers all-star Freddie Freeman, ranges to his right to field the ball, and Ax thinks to himself, *Just go!* He races to cover first, standard pitcher's-fielding-practice routine. My breath catches as I recall his clanked basket catches during pregame, his brand new baseball glove. And here's Freeman's overhand feed—firm, accurate, professional—and Ax thinks, *OK, just catch it with your hands. Now find the base. Aaaaand we're good.* Two outs. He and Freeman share a knowing look, a quick grin.

Britain's third batter, pinch-hitter Alex Crosby, swings at Ax's first pitch—a hard sinker—and lines out softly to shortstop.

There it is. A quick, clean, 12-pitch inning.

We don't best the gods. But we might coauthor their final entry in the ledger.

Ax steps off the mound and pounds his fist in his glove a couple times. As he crosses the foul line he looks up toward his family, his kids, where they're on their feet and cheering. He raises his glove and waves. The moment lingers, and then he disappears into the dugout.

———

Two days later, before Canada's game with Colombia, his elbow is still red and swollen, the joint full of fluid. He can neither touch his own shoulder nor straighten his arm completely. If he'd been on a normal rehab progression, he would have been throwing low-intensity live-at-bats on a back field at someone's spring training complex. Instead, he'd dialed up 12 max effort pitches. His arm didn't react well. He won't pitch again in the World Baseball Classic. Canada goes into the final day of pool play with a 2-1 record but they fall to Team Mexico, who's already beaten the US team and will ultimately advance to the semifinal against Japan.

So what's next for John Axford?

Some relaxation and catching up on movies at home, first. Then he'll be in Milwaukee again this spring, for the Film Festival.

And after that?

There's been discussion, sure. Coaching or a front-office gig or maybe something outside baseball entirely that involves lenses and shutter speeds and a creative eye. But who knows? Ax isn't even retired from playing yet. To be honest, he's not the kind of guy who will need or want to say it so definitively. None of his favorite films end so declaratively, after all.

If this were a Hollywood movie, it might end with a shot of J.B. and Jameson coming home from school to be surprised by the rescue dog their dad has promised them once he quits playing. But if this were a film in the style of John Axford's favorites, its dénouement would be more enigmatic—something evocative and open-ended and absolutely unyielding.

So, it's morning in the empty ballpark at Peoria Sports Complex in Arizona, spring training home of the Seattle Mariners. Oh, the rhythm of this quiet garden, the grounds crew at their meticulous, loving tasks. A pushbroom returns scattered clay to the base paths. The batting practice cage appears from its hidden alcove, the grounds crew herding it like a giant furtive turtle. Back inside the Mariners' clubhouse a ping pong battle is underway, pitcher versus outfielder. English and Spanish fly as their teammates cheer and rag and goad. Soon, the calculating front-office types will levy fate. But not yet. And outside, the Canadian buses have arrived, parking beyond the fence in the right-field corner. The red-clad players slowly filter in and lounge in the outfield grass, bullshitting. Here comes the dirt-splattered Workman, its gas fumes, its bed laden with rakes, brooms, the ground crew's tamp. Up on the concourse, stadium workers in their matching shirts have gathered for marching orders. The fryers come on at the funnel cake booth atop the berm, and now music flits somewhere. The manager, the old ballplayer, has joined his guys in the outfield—he leans on a fungo bat and tells stories. The Workman drags the infield smooth, dust gently unspooling in the slanted plane of still-rising sunlight. The ballplayers in right field circle and stretch and Ax is among them, and that's it.

The Secrets of a "Homeless Influencer"

LAUREN ABUNASSAR

The sky over Detroit's long-shuttered Herman Kiefer Hospital is dense and dark, punctured only by the dim light of a few weak street lamps. Passing cars fill the night with a thready and echoing roar, not unlike the illusion of an ocean contained in a shell. Every now and then, their headlights needle through the darkness and Shamseddeen "Sham" Moussaoui has to turn off his headlamp and duck out of view.

What Sham needs is not light. It is luck.

There are, after all, security guards posted around the hospital's perimeter. As he holds his camera in front of him, hands shaky but voice steady, Sham whispers into the recorder, "Hopefully there's nobody walking around. They're going to be on the lookout for me. Moreso, they know the terrain."

The terrain—toppled traffic cones, ramparts of barbed-wire and chain-link, padlocked doors and marooned construction vehicles. Somewhere, a Jeep is making lazy but dutiful circles around the parking lot, looking for trespassers. Looking for Sham. And then, there is some luck. After scaling a bit of slackened barbed-wire, Sham finds a cracked door and is able to squeeze his way inside the hospital.

The corridors are crowded with construction supplies and trash. Cracks web the white brick walls, a firehose hangs lazily from the door like the shed skin of a snake. Two bicycles are propped against the wall, tools laid out beside them as if someone was repairing the chain or refilling a tire before being called away.

This is the nature of abandoned buildings. Often, they dwell in a state of limbo. There are the shadowy traces of care and life but there is also the fast-eclipsing hand of disrepair. The hospital, for Sham, is an adventure. But it's also a monument to just how sad forgotten things appear. The histories that lie hidden and, too often, unexamined.

Sham pauses briefly by the bikes. "Holy crap," he says. He has made it inside.

It hasn't even been ten minutes when the unnerving echo of barking surges down the hall. It is hard to tell if the dog is a stray or another form of security. But these questions become less urgent than the fast-approaching sound of snarling. Suddenly, Sham is in view, his camera shaking dangerously as he runs away full-speed from the dog. The chaos of film pivots between shaky shots of Sham's gray gym shorts, his black sneakers, concrete stairs, and the surround-sound of his uncertain panting as the dog gives chase. He is trying to narrate for his internet audience as he makes his cinematic getaway.

Today he insists that he wasn't scared. He never is when he does this.

Huck Finn had his river, Kerouac his road, Ishmael his sea. Sham has his abandoned buildings. All 21 of them. Eighteen abandoned, two under construction, one still operational. Ten cities. Thirty-five hours of exploration.

You could say he's a man with many names and just as many lives. Digitally, he is a compressed "iamshamtheman," on Instagram. He reduces his biography on YouTube to: "Unconventional Journey & Rare Explorations." Sometimes he calls himself the Road Trip Renegade.

He keeps a digital map that tracks his travels— a thin blue line charting the path he took from Jacksonville, through Charlotte, Morgantown, Pittsburgh, Dearborn. He drove across the country six times. He hit forty states. He snuck inside a children's hospital under construction in West Virginia. A sanatorium in Cleveland. The old Heinz Factory in Pittsburgh. He has hidden in meat lockers and behind filing cabinets, trying to avoid security looking for trespassers. He has been caught by trees while escaping from police into the forest after exploring Forest Fair Mall in Cincinnati. He has faced guard dogs and squatters, his own demons even—crouched in the shadows with the detritus of what has been left behind. His journeys verge on Odyssean. But it's not home he's looking for; it's something harder to pinpoint. The opportunity to explore the abandoned has a siren-like pull. There is a story behind everything, after all.

When his car broke down in November 2021, he flew from Detroit to Las Vegas, using a plane ticket his friend Abe bought him. He had three bags. They were all stolen when he arrived at the airport. "At that moment, all I had was everything I was wearing. I had my wallet. I had my cell phone." Maybe it's weird, he says. But again, he wasn't scared.

He felt fearless again when he left Las Vegas to get to Chicago in October 2022.

He's a fan of the Stoics. Marcus Aurelius and Seneca are taped to the digital walls of his online profiles. It is in this philosophy, he says, where his absence of fear draws some explanation. "The whole idea is to literally focus on only the next step," he says. "So even if everybody took everything I own on planet Earth, I would still be calm. And that is what I taught myself. It's like, nothing is too big to overcome."

<hr>

Sham wakes up surrounded by a copse of calligraphic oak trees. The nearby Des Plaines River runs like a green lung along the border of the nature preserve where he sleeps, the mummy bag he bought cheap, a chrysalis-like shelter against weather that sometimes swings well below zero.

Aside from the weather, it's not totally unlike his set up in Vegas—where he'd dumpster dive for food if he maxed out his monthly EBT allowance. It was easier to find food this way in Michigan. Whole pizzas, frozen supermarket pies, a Gatorade or some discarded buffalo wings. In Vegas, it was trickier. In Chicago, trickier still.

He uses his SNAP benefits to buy baggies of crystallized ginger for energy, huge tubs of spinach, cans of sardines and tuna and chicken because, joking that "you've got to diversify your meats. And no, that's not my advice for women." It's a balancing act that sometimes leaves him out of benefits only part way through the month. He knows what it's like to go hungry.

Sham likes parks because he likes getting some distance from the homeless. Homelessness, after all, comes with a certain set of stereotypes he's trying to avoid. "My joke is the two most common homeless questions are 'do you have X? Or do you know somebody who has X?'" he says. He faced this when, one night, he woke up to a twenty dollar bill being shoved in his face, accompanied by a voice asking for crystal meth. And in Chicago when he got on the train to shelter from the cold, he says that "This older crackhead guy was sleeping next to me. He wakes up, looks at me. He's like you got any change? I'm like, No. Then he got pissed off. He's like, 'Every stop has an ATM…' He got in my face and tried to block my way out. I had to pull out my knife." It was his first night wandering the transit system while he figured out where to go next.

The unfortunate part of being who he is, Sham says, involves the labor of correction. He has to correct the story people assign to him because he is homeless. This is not a challenge unique to him. But what people don't understand is the way he has, to a certain degree, elected to this path. He has a hard time imagining himself traveling to see his buildings, he says, if he did have a home. He has a hard time imagining a home that wouldn't feel like a prison.

When he wakes up, he usually goes to McDonalds to buy a $1 order of fries. He wants to keep finding work, temporary gigs that will help save up for a car and restore his travels, looking for his next abandoned building. When he's fully woken up, he'll head over to Panera Bread where he's a member of the monthly Sip Club. He'll get coffee, use the WiFi to post videos, update his social media. Sometimes people will approach him, again, with a specific story in mind. "There's a group of old ladies talking," he says, remembering one such interaction back in a Panera in Vegas. One of them asked if he was traveling—a cautious disguise for the question she really wanted to ask. "I know what she meant. And I'm just straight up— No, I'm homeless… They're always shocked."

In the face of this shock, the woman gave him a $100 bill. He tried to refuse it but she was an adamant do-gooder. So too was her friend who came up after her and gave Sham another $100. "They're not coincidences anymore," Sham says. "I've gone through too many of these months where things just happened; they're meant for something."

Sham tells me about a childhood friend, Ebrahim "Abe" Siala, in his native Corvallis, Oregon. He calls him weekly and they talk, sometimes, for upwards of eight hours. Recently, Abe had an idea. "Maybe look at it this way," he told Sham, "you were put in a place so that others can do good deeds. I was like that's a real interesting perspective. You know, I'm allowing others to do goodness, in a way."

Sham is an instrument and an agent. He receives the good and he tries to push the good back out.

One of his followers on Reddit—ChargerGirl82 because in Sham's world, a digital name is as valid as a Christian one—got in touch while living out of her car in San Diego where it's illegal to do so. Deaf, she didn't hear when the cops came knocking on her window one day. And so when they broke the glass, she didn't know what to do. She was only 20 when she first reached out, a fact that took Sham by surprise recently as he thought the 82 in her handle was her birth year. She reached out to Sham, first, to talk about donating plasma. "Happy 5 months!," she wrote to him near the anniversary of his homelessness. "You have such a cute face."

Again, the idea of the secret story became an organizing part of their interactions. Rachel, the real ChargerGirl82, aged out of foster care. She did a big search. Found her birth mother across the country. Went to see her birth mother and, through a series of disasters, ended up having to call CPS on her.

"I mean, this person has gone through a lot of suffering, you know, to be just cast out, given nothing," Sham says. "I feel in a weird way, not to be delusional, but that I was meant to kind of be a voice for these things… To make people feel human again."

Life goes on. Rachel replaced her window with tarp. Started offering to work for free just to prove that she could work. Sham became a pseudo big brother to her, guiding her through the intricacies of survival. Maybe one day she'd come meet him wherever he was and they'd go exploring together.

There are so many more stories to tell. Sham wants to be a part of that.

There are the people who live in the tunnels back in Vegas for example. The homeless that huddle inside the 24-hour train-route to O'Hare, sleeping for an hour and half only to wake up when the train reaches its endpoint, swap cars, repeat all over again. There's the parking garages. Gyms, stairwells, ATM cubicles. Sham went to a medical office recently that was undergoing renovation. He stayed for a few days, rejoicing in the luxury of heat, power, five indoor toilets. Then he got caught and had to move on again. "In a weird way, it's like I'm channeling some sort of criminal instinct in terms of how to survive. I noticed a big part of urban exploring is being able to adapt knowing how to survive. Finding these little tricks. Like right now, my eyes are so conditioned to always scanning buildings, scanning for places I can sleep…"

Everywhere he finds people who are lost. Also abandoned. It'd be cool to go down into those Vegas tunnels, for example, he says. An adventure of another kind. "To get life stories and start doing portraits on them. To try to bring information and bring people back to the light, so to speak. Because I didn't have any of that."

A construction site is a ruin in reverse.

This is a lesson social and cultural geographer and urban explorer Dr. Bradley L. Garrett learned firsthand. With his doctoral thesis focused on a community of urban explorers, Garrett remembers Mark Explores approaching him about sneaking into a skyscraper. He didn't get the appeal. After all, the skyscraper was just under construction. It didn't have a story yet.

He had spent his time following explorers drawn to the decay of a place. Ruination as a memorial—history tucked between ragged fence lines and broken windows, dry rotted floors and rusted metal frames. But then Explores said something that hit—"We're the story now."

So Garrett joined in. And from there, his exploring community would go into skyscrapers to photograph them as the floors were added, inching higher and higher above the skyline, understanding the structure of the finished building before even the developers. "I think what happens for a lot of people is that it began with an interest in places," he says. Reconfiguring one's mind to store blueprints of forgotten sectors and tunnels, buildings people don't yet see as beautiful or have stopped seeing as beautiful, it all involves an interest in that which is hidden. "Carrying around that secret knowledge is very empowering."

Traveling with explorers around Europe, he remembers weeks spent sleeping in abandoned buildings, traveling from place to place. Just like Sham. The question of urban exploration and homelessness becomes a chicken before the egg type of paradox. The passion for exploring could push one to homelessness. And homelessness could certainly push one to explore. In each case, it becomes an issue of survival and how we tender this through movement.

Transiency unfolds, according to Garrett, like something out of a China Miéville novel where the world is composed of two cities on top of one another. "People in one city can't see people in the other city," he says. "And they have totally different cultural contexts… We just had this completely upside down agenda of, you know, climbing through windows and sleeping in boarded up buildings. And we had a lot of conversations on those trips about why we're paying rent."

The world is full of abandoned buildings and abandoned people. Garrett remembers the base jumper he came across while scaling Heron Tower in London. He leapt off the side wall, opened his parachute, landed, and ran off into the night.

And then there was the campsite Garrett and his team discovered in an abandoned Soviet Military base in Poland. Hidden in a dense forest with a treacherous circuit of dirt roads and an intricate network of buildings, the sudden image of a tent was a mind boggling prospect. There was laundry hanging. There was a mirror for shaving. "And we just realized, like, this is someone's home."

For weeks, Garrett and friends spun secret histories for the mystery camper. Garrett, with his PhD and his postdoctoral fellowship at Oxford, envied the squatter. After all, he had a whole military base to himself. The feeling of disconnection from society is not always a burden. Sometimes it's a liberation. And it's a liberation perfectly paralleled in urban exploration. Permission to enter a space tempers the excitement of it. Discovery of a place exudes power. Evasion is accompanied by euphoria. A crime is not always about what you can take or destroy but about the thrill of being able to walk away at the end of it.

In Sham's case, though Garrett has never met him or heard of him, his story of self-removal makes some sense. "If you've experienced trauma," he says, "if you've experienced alienation and frustration, there would be a huge draw to just going into the drains under Las Vegas and vanishing into a secret world that you have control over…"

Corvallis, Oregon sits along the eastern edge of the Pacific Coast Range. Snow is rare but often, thick shelves of fog cover the verdant green landscape like sheets of tulle. Sham grew up in the city in low-income housing with seven brothers and sisters. His mother immigrated from Algeria and his father from Morocco.

Today, Sham tracks their passage to America the way many children of diasporas do—one family member followed another. First a few uncles. Then grandparents. Cousins. In Corvallis, Sham says, assimilation became tricky. "The theme," he says of his upbringing, "was that society is evil. The outside, the American system is evil."

Piecing the story together, there's not much Sham doesn't trace back to his upbringing. Secret worlds shelled themselves out behind closed bedroom doors in his childhood home. These bedrooms were not abandoned buildings but there was the same mordant tinge that comes with life as it vanishes. Everyone withdrew from each other, he says. "I didn't have those fishing trips. I didn't go out to a restaurant. We never went as a family to eat out in my entire life. Never went to a movie theater… It has to have a psychological effect."

The penchant for wandering was present in his childhood as well. He began walking the streets, the western sky flat and dark above him like a sheet of construction paper. He began getting into trouble in school. Teachers were perplexed: "you could be a leader," they told him. And then one day, a kid made a racist remark on the bus and Sham broke his nose. He was expelled and spent a few days in juvenile detention.

Still in Corvallis today, Sham's childhood friend Abe remembers Sham as a sparring partner and de facto little brother. Abe got Sham into Jiujitsu and the two would spar in the inner prayer room of their local mosque. It was a hobby Sham ran with, leveraging his fighting skills into a career as an amateur MMA fighter. In 2011, Sham was making promises to a local Oregon paper to "control my opponent and impose my will," while preparing for a fight against lightweight champion Justin Mark at the Chinook Winds Casino Resort.

In those post-fight interviews, it's as if a pressure valve has been released. His eyes winnow down to a thrilled squint, his smile breaks open like an egg. Blood pools around his cheekbone where a bruise is already forming. His chest bears a tattoo of the emblem on an Algerian flag—his mother's homeland. Even as a victor, his past is something he wears.

"The more I think about it," says Sham's childhood friend, Abe, "I feel like what he's doing, he has to do it. What he's doing, it can't be done any other way."

In a world far away from Sham's, there is something even Abe recognizes in Sham's wandering. He was there to watch his power evolve into his downfall and he remembers one of the last in-person conversations he had with Sham in his backyard in Corvallis. Sham opened up to him about his own mental health, his struggle with bipolar disorder and addiction. And he opened up about what homelessness was really like. "He was talking about the brain and how—and I can relate to this—because you don't have someone to talk to constantly, your brain just wires differently. So I guess what he was communicating was the idea that these people out there alone, these people don't have anybody to talk to… and it sort of turns them into a zombie."

Tucked inside this translation is some rationale for Sham's exploration and his social media exploits. Don't we all long for a sense of community? Don't we all have something we want to escape? Don't we all want something that restores some illusion of control that life, in all its prevailing unfairnesses, has taken from us?

Again and again, Abe insists that "I just want to emphasize how big a dichotomy there is between the Sham that was and the Sham that is. It's just day and night."

As proud as he is of Sham's growth, there's a simple confession to make: "I worry."

Sometimes, there isn't much more to say.

Luckless, life becomes a series of close calls. Before Chicago, in Vegas, Sham hadn't eaten in three days.

More urgently, Rachel. She went missing for a while. Unable to get in touch, he planned his own search for her, preparing to call Walmarts across California to see if she might be in one of their parking lots.

When he finally tracked her down, he listened to her story about being stabbed while sleeping in her own park some 330 miles away. Maybe someone had asked her for something and she couldn't hear them so they stabbed her. "That is the difficulty with not being able to hear," she writes to him. "Sometimes you just have to make guesses about how things happen." Sham listens to it all. Together, they are linked by their acutely attuned ability to just keep going. Rachel's kidney was pierced but she only spent one night in the hospital because she wanted to get back to her search for work.

Sham had his own ER stay recently when he spent a few summer weeks recycling garbage in a small warehouse. Cinched inside a column of arid heat, Sham had to eventually call an ambulance to take him to the hospital with severe hydration. These stories they share become a vessel for confronting life. For saying one has survived and keeps surviving.

When Rachel resurfaced, "She was excited," Sham says. "And that's why I came to Chicago."

According to Sham, Rachel was in hospice here with late-stage cancer, surrounded by caseworkers and healthcare staff buffeting his attempts to get in touch. In hospice, Rachel would send Sham updates about her worsening condition, the nose injuries she was enduring from congestion, a rotating cocktail of painkillers, the enduring struggle to breathe. Sham looked into experimental trials, alternative treatments, alternative facilities. He insists the staff wouldn't tell Rachel the name of the hospice center. All Sham could see was a state of Illinois badge on a nurse in an innocuous photo Rachel once sent him. She hadn't been outside in five or six months.

"Rachel's garbage to the system," Sham explains bitterly. He senses a conspiracy in that as soon as he started trying to pin down plans to come and visit, he was disconnected by her care team. "I got through one time a couple of weeks ago," he explains, "a woman picked up and it kind of sounded like her caseworker. And when I'm like, you know, is Rachel around, it's an immediate hangup. I called right back. And then nobody answered. And then I was blocked."

From there: Her email was blocked. Her Reddit deactivated. Messages unreturned. "It's 100% clear there's something really dark about this whole system of just rushing her through towards death, not having any resistance from outside forces."

Because Medicaid will not provide coverage to you in two states at the same time, he took a big gamble and went off his medication when he made the move to Chicago to try and find her. It wasn't long after he arrived that Rachel disappeared again. "I started to lose my way, because, again, mental health," he says. Her absence was a crushing blow. "I was just kind of going through the motions…just kind of wandering."

He met another homeless man who was also born in Oregon. The coincidence buoyed him in the face of his growing depression. His new friend found them another kind of abandoned shelter—a three bedroom empty apartment in Dekalb where Sham was able to stay for a week before he woke up one morning to commotion and a voice saying, "you're not even supposed to be here." He went back to his park. He rode the trains again when the weather got bad. He used GoodRX to get back on his medication, $86 out of pocket. When his camping gear was stolen from its hiding place in the woods when he was out for the day, he found an office building open to blood donations 24 hours a day. He hides in the hallway and has been camped there for the past month.

"It's the monotony that makes me restless," Sham says. "And it's a sign, I find it's a sign within my body. Something has to change." He's giving it a month before he gives up on the possibility of closure with Rachel. He'll save enough money to invest in film and survival equipment and then who knows? Maybe he'll hop a freight train. Chicago, he says, is the train hub of America after all. Maybe he'll get as far out as Washington where he wants to take some work on a friend's new farm. Maybe he'll go to Detroit. Maybe he'll go to D.C. to see the RFK stadium, do some exploring before its demolition is complete.

His next paycheck he wants to buy some new video equipment to do some exploring in Chicago; he refuses to leave without this. At least two places, he says. Grain silos first—something he's never explored but that dot the Illinois landscape as regularly as vertebrae on spine.

"Part of me believes I could have saved her," he says of the guilt and sorrow that needles him as he wonders where Rachel could be.

Still, there are issues that, when brought up, irritate him deeply. He's never video chatted with Rachel. Because she is deaf, phone conversations have also been unrealistic. When Rachel was in San Diego, she assured Sham she wanted him involved in her care. They were going to coordinate paperwork with Sham so that her information could be shared with him. Right before this, Sham says, he was blocked. Sham shares the name of the high school Rachel supposedly attended in Chicago. But their alumni database lists no one who corresponds with her name, and a school staff member Sham spoke to recently had never heard of Rachel.

He angrily rejects a cruel possibility—Rachel might not be who she says she is. More than anything, he resents the possibility that people might not hear about her story, so extraordinary it seems downright unbelievable. Then again, he resents the possibility that people might not hear his story either. "Nothing is wasted," he says of the time he has spent in Chicago looking for her. The trick is to find a way to use your story for something bigger.

––––––––

Once, Sham was walking to the bus stop when he was attacked. Three men threading through traffic on the strip closed in on Sham, screaming for him to hand over his bags. He still regrets the fact that he wasn't able to get it on camera.

And though he recalls the story with a thrilled pride that he's survived, in the moment, he didn't have much choice. "I'm guarding my entire life," he says. Of course he didn't hand over his bags. As the fight ensued, a tangled scuffle backlit by the churlish glow of neon lights, revelation dawned on Sham— there must be a hundred people right there in person, just watching. As he frantically mimed "phone, phone," to his audience, he grew more and more perplexed as to why no one would help him. "The only call that went through was made by me," he says soberly.

In this way, Sham embodies a complicated set of contradictions. He is passionate about his presence online, advocating for what it really means to be homeless. But he is also rankled by the moments in which he is victimized by spectator culture. He lives his life publicly but he has his secrets too. He has an unchecked optimism and a desire to find his community but he's also a self-described lone wolf. When he explores his abandoned buildings, he always explores alone.

Every now and then, he speaks of loneliness. But these confessions are absorbed by a firmly held belief that luck will always return. The misfortune will equalize, another kismet gift will come along at just the right moment.

"Zeno went through a shipwreck, and he swam to shore," Sham explains, returning to his philosophers. "Edison's factory burned down.

And they looked at this as an opportunity of rebirth. There was no complaining. They're like, it's done. All that stuff is done. Let me focus on the present… Present means gift. So you're being gifted this moment. Let me let me use it for something."

Something Sham believes: No one else has recorded and posted footage from inside the long abandoned Veterans Affairs Hospital in Pittsburgh. But Sham has.

Just off the Allegheny River, the building has been closed since 2013. In October 2021, less than two months shy of losing his car and becoming fully homeless, he risked federal trespassing and military police patrol just to get a glimpse at the hospital. He describes it as a mini city, removed from the world, and still largely lit. The aerial view of the 168 acre medical campus looks not unlike the box fort city a kid might string up in their living room.

Inside, there are gessoed floors and drop down ceilings. An old bowling alley and a couple nature portraits on the waterlogged wall of the old canteen. A chapel with colored glass windows. A cafeteria and a kitchen with peeling ceilings and an "incoming delivery" sign still posted to the wall. These are the rooms people used to sleep in. These are the tables where they ate. The chapels where they prayed. The labs where they studied new PTSD treatments, the basement where they did laundry, the corridor that filters the light in chunks through the blue-tinged windows.

"When I find myself there," Sham says, "alone in a seven-story lit hospital, and I'm standing there in the hallway by myself, like, this is unbelievable. Imagine that…I'm just in my mind, I'm envisioning other people experiencing this through the lens of my GoPro in that first person view, which is what I want to recreate. Just that amazing feeling of being in this place alone."

For all its criminal connotations, trespass in Old French means "to pass over." This is the act of exploration, also. To pass over what is gone and what is left. Who Sham has been and who he may or may not become. Standing alone in a hallway, marveling at the light, feeling some alloyed sensation of thrill and peace.

In just two days, he will be a couple miles further down the river exploring an abandoned factory. But for a quiet moment, in a place he should not be, he is happy to stand still. He is not afraid of anything.

POLITICS & CITY LIFE

Labor, Solidarity, and Nursing

EVA ROSENFELD

"Why do nurses strike?"

A nurse and state union leader named Nadine Furlong delivered a speech with this title at a 1984 ethics conference sponsored by the University of Michigan. Furlong was exasperated with the question, or at least the underlying accusation, which seemed actually to be "Why do nurses strike when the right to strike conflicts with the duty to care?" Such an inquiry was laced with "erroneous assumptions," she said. It assumed that the nurse has duties in the hospital that transcend the standard employee-employer relationship. It assumed that these "unsubstantiated duties" negated the basic societal right of employees to challenge chronically unsafe workplaces: in her view, the true source of harm to patients.

Asserting this right has been the basis of the nursing labor movement, which has grown in strength over the past two years. Nurses, mostly those in unions affiliated with the country's largest nursing labor organization, National Nurses United, have organized strikes and labor actions across the country in response to ever more debilitating work conditions amidst the pandemic. Healthcare workers made up almost half of striking workers last year, mainly nurses and lower-paid support staff. They emphasized demands for "safe staffing" and protested "chronically understaffed" workplaces, where caregivers continually find themselves torn between patients, forced by time constraints to deliver compromised care.

In summer of 2022, nurses at the University of Michigan were particularly understaffed, stretched thinner because the hospital had laid off 738 support staff early in the pandemic to counter projected income loss. The hospital rebounded the next calendar year, profiting millions, but never rehired the workers. Short-staffed, managers enforced "mandatory overtime," creating an uncompensated on-call system to fill gaps on the hospital floor.

It was the kind of desperate scenario that pushes nurses to the picket lines. The University of Michigan Professional Nurses Council (UMPNC), an affiliate of the Michigan Nurses Association at the state level and National Nurses United at the national level, authorized a "work stoppage"—it is illegal for public employees to formally strike in Michigan—and sued their employer. They ultimately won contract language that enforced nurse-to-patient ratios and ended mandatory overtime, clauses they hoped would return the burden of staffing the hospital to management. It was a solid victory on a set of issues that had plagued their workplace since at least the time Furlong took to the stage to correct the record on union nurses' motives.

In fact, the problems University of Michigan picketed over in summer 2022 were remarkably similar to those they described in the 1980s. Responding to a 1981 survey over work conditions, nurses wrote:

"We're chronically understaffed."

"We have much mandatory overtime, and very sick patients. And NO extra staff to call upon in emergencies."

"We are tremendously overworked to the danger point of unsafe patient care."

"I hate to watch competent, highly skilled people leave out of sheer overwork and frustration; to save their very sanity."

Any time a hospital lacks the capacity to care for all the patients who need treatment, newspapers tend to attribute the problem to a nationwide nursing shortage, as they did in the 1980s and again during the early days of the pandemic. Nurses' unions today have been quick to counter that there is not a shortage of nurses, but rather of desirable workplaces. A March 2022 study from the American Nurses Foundation found that over half of U.S. nurses are considering leaving their jobs "due primarily to insufficient staffing, work negatively affecting health and well-being, and inability to deliver quality care," while other studies have placed this figure as high as 90 percent. The labor supply in nursing varies dramatically across regions, and sometimes it can impact hospitals' ability to hire, but understaffing persists in every kind of hospital, regardless of the labor market.   Heidi Shierholz, president of the Economic Policy Institute, writes of a ubiquitous dynamic in which "Employers post their too-low wages, can't find workers to fill jobs at that pay level, and claim they're facing a labor shortage."

Nurses share many complaints with workers in general, whose mass discontent has collectively sparked the "Great Resignation" and a spike in labor organizing. But unlike employees of most industries, who have organized around their own physical and economic precarity as they try to stay alive and afloat in the pandemic, nurses' unions, with their clarion call for "safe staffing," point to the precarity of their patients as evidence of a broken system.

Why *do* nurses strike? In Michigan, nurses' unions formed in the shadow of auto unions, but faced a unique set of challenges as they defined their values and struggled for labor rights. Many of these obstacles were imposed by gendered stereotypes about nurses' work; others stemmed from the emotional and moral issues endemic to caregiving. After all, a nurse fighting for a better workplace faces a different human equation than a trade worker. A nurses' union represents its workers, too, but "we have that third person," she says, "a third piece in our union that others don't"—the patient. "And your decisions, how you can do the work that you are accountable in your profession to do, affects that person's life, and their future."

The discontented nurses of 1981 were a new kind of healthcare worker, armed with new labor rights and fresh insights from the feminist movement. They were also confronting a new kind of hospital. After the passage of Medicaid and Medicare in 1965, hospitals expanded across the country as insurance payments flowed into a healthcare system for which demand was steadily increasing. Healthcare consumption grew for many reasons, including an aging population. But in manufacturing hubs like Michigan or Pennsylvania, writes the labor historian Gabriel Winant, this growth was due in large part to the social dynamics of industrial decline.

As industrial labor won power in the mid-century, workers gained economic security, though much of their earnings came in the form of fringe benefits, like health insurance. As Winant explains in his book *The Next Shift*, which demonstrates how a contracting industrial economy gave way to a caregiving economy in the Rust Belt, these workers were able to take advantage of the healthcare system to meet basic social needs, like elder care and disability treatment. It was "a way of expanding the footprint of the welfare state without actually having to win any political victories," Winant said in an interview.

Industries that depend on direct human service, like healthcare, childcare, and education, have certain fundamental properties, he explains. They are labor-intensive, they are in many ways more art than science, and, within them, there are hard, human limits to how much productivity can increase. And so, as healthcare services expanded from the late 1960s into the early 1980s, their growth was unavoidably labor-intensive. It was in hospitals' interest to hire fast to meet demand. At the same time, they faced mounting external pressure from regulators to cut costs.

By the late 1970s, the federal government had begun to panic over the rising cost of healthcare, which bureaucrats blamed on the "overutilization" of care. The Carter administration deputized regional planning councils called Health Systems Agencies (HSAs) to reduce services. This convoluted regulatory regime was never terribly effective, not least because HSAs often had goals that contradicted their official mandate. Local officials serving on these councils, for instance, saw that hospitals were becoming crucial sites of employment and investment in deindustrializing areas that otherwise faced a sharp decline in economic activity. Healthcare costs have been viewed nationally as a fiscal problem, but health care inflation "represented, ironically, a political *solution* to the ravages of deindustrialization," writes Winant.

By the mid-80s, cost-cutting would radically restructure the hospital environment. But even by the late 1970s, with austerity politics in the air, hospitals anxiously searched for savings in their growing wage bills. They lowered pay, but also assigned more patients to proportionately fewer workers, and redistributed technical tasks to lower-paid tiers of employees.

Nurses were an easy target. Until the mid-20th century, hospitals "were just not used to paying for nursing care," says nursing historian Julie Fairman in an interview. Even after the days of religious nursing missions, hospitals depended largely on uncompensated nursing students in their training schools to make up their workforces. "Hospitals have always used nurses as ways to not just remain solvent, but to keep their economic overview as good as possible," she says.

Most healthcare workers in the U.S. gained the right to collectively bargain in 1974, when an amendment to the National Labor Relations Act removed an exemption of the nonprofit healthcare industry from labor relations statutes. Yet in most states, including Michigan, nurses embraced this development slowly. In the 1980s, collective bargaining still remained "a subject of controversy" and "somewhat foreign to many nurses," wrote Patricia Ibbotson, RN, in a 1981 issue of *The Michigan Nurse*, the publication of the Michigan Nurses Association. The profession was bogged down in its historical identity—what the American Nurses Association (ANA) then called the "you'll get your reward in heaven" philosophy.

The 1974 amendments fueled fierce debates over the value of unionism. Across Michigan, nurses were torn between "the conflicting ideologies of a service-humanitarian orientation sometimes called 'Nightingalism,'" after the famous nineteenth-century nurse, and "the desire to be assured economic security and recognition as a professional," wrote one Detroit nurse, Phyllis Brenner, in 1983. What did it mean for a profession originating in religious volunteerism, long predicated on the uncompensated or undercompensated caring labor of women, to reverse course and make demands on their employers, even to strike?

Pro-labor attitudes spread as nurses took cues from the women's movement to stand up for themselves in the workplace. Throughout the 1980s, columnists in the Michigan Nurse attempted to raise the consciousness of their colleagues. "Women, including nurses, have been told power isn't 'nice.' This perception is inaccurate. Nurses are the key component in the healthcare delivery system in this country. They have the potential for great power," wrote Ibbotson in 1981. "Collective bargaining is a useful adjunct in achieving a power base for nursing and a tool for professional growth."

Dozens of other nurses penned similar appeals. Articles prepared nurses for grievance and arbitration processes, informed them of their rights under OSHA, and tried to rouse what was widely viewed as an apolitical group, describing tiers of participation from "apathetic" to "gladiator." "Examine nursing curricula and note the lack of political content. However unintentional, conformity and docility have frequently been the affective student ideals fostered by faculty," wrote two RNs in 1983, a time when 98 percent of nurses were women. But reconciling the identities of "caregiver" and "laborer" remained a difficult task, even for unabashedly pro-union nurses.

These issues came to a head in 1981, when the University of Michigan nurses held their first "work stoppage," lasting 23 days. Just over half of the hospital RNs walked out. A report created after the strike by outside consultants, hired by hospital management to conduct a "healing project," documents the reactions of nurses from both sides of the picket line. Nurses who worked through the strike accused strikers of perpetuating a "negative uncaring image." Both sides called the others "traitors."

They sparred with particular animation over the meaning of "professionalism," a term that proved flexible enough to represent any view of collective bargaining; those who supported it and those who opposed it both claimed to be fighting for their professional values. Unionism was not exactly popular among nurses, and its critics tended to take the position that professionals didn't join unions, that collective bargaining was a blue-collar tactic belonging to the trade unions, which, in Michigan, always meant auto workers.

Nadine Furlong, in her 1984 speech, represented the opposite view: "The argument to work it out 'professionally' flies in the face of fact," she said. "Nurses have acted 'professional', been 'dedicated' and had a just cause, for 100 years. During this time they have remained economically exploited and professionally liable for unsafe nursing care of patients due to inadequate working conditions."

Still, even striking nurses felt conflicted about their identities:

"We didn't really act like *labor*—the strike was quiet and peaceful."

"No matter how hard I try, I can't feel like an auto worker or coal miner."

"Professionalism" took on contradictory meanings because it is, in Winant's terms, "a contradictory phenomenon"— a designation for workers who participate in "some of the functions of management," or at least exert some control over who gets to enter their profession. The socialist writer Barbara Ehrenreich and journalist Dierdre English criticized the drive to professionalize nursing altogether. At best, they wrote, it failed to challenge the gendered hierarchy of medicine. "At worst, it is sexist itself, deepening the division among women health workers and bolstering a hierarchy controlled by men."

Like their detractors, union nurses used the term "professionalism" to distinguish their work from a less credentialed tier—not industrial labor, but "feminine vocations" like unpaid caregiving, domestic work, and lower-paid healthcare work. They wanted to stop being treated like a catch-all profession, the unofficial mothers of the hospital, expected to pick up what was left on the floor. In 1981, the UMPNC won a "Professional Nursing" clause. It defined what university nurses' duties included and, maybe more importantly, excluded. Even today Michigan nurses point to this contract language to decline when they are asked, for instance, to start taking out the trash.

Pro-union nurses wanted just as much as anti-union nurses to be seen as professionals, but they saw unionism as a path to professionalism, not its antithesis. Real professionalism, to them, meant autonomy in the daily operations of nursing. This included higher nurse-to-patient ratios, control over how the hospital floor was staffed, and flexibility to make clinical decisions without a doctor's supervision. A good contract, they believed, was the only mechanism with any teeth to gain these things, plus better pay.

Still, these concerns, so closely tied to the act of caregiving, felt distant from the goals of classic trade unionism. Striking may have been necessary, but that did not make the decision to leave a patient at the bedside less fraught or painful. Many of those who walked out in 1981 echoed the feelings of one nurse, who reported, "I was so frightened by walking a picket line and yet I couldn't seem to figure out any other way to get better working conditions. I just kept crying all night before it happened." Margo Baron, who founded the UMPNC, was known to remark, "Nurses never go on strike for money."

Within the nursing establishment, unions had an uneasy foothold. Both the MNA and its national counterpart, the American Nurses Association (ANA), were "professional organizations" whose leadership consisted mostly of nurse higher-ups—executives or educators who did not provide direct care. The difference between a professional organization and a union had always been murky, but depended mainly on the familiar distinctions of status and expertise. ANA had been officially sympathetic to collective bargaining since the 1940s but maintained a no-strike position until 1968. The MNA, meanwhile, had a small labor arm with limited representative power whose goals often clashed with those of managerial nurses at the helm.

As deindustrialization eroded the membership of Michigan auto unions, some tried to recruit health workers into their ranks. But many nurses felt that these invitations were themselves a threat to the ideal of "control over practice." Joan Guy, an MNA executive, chided nurses who wanted to take advantage of the clout and resources of established unions. They were already struggling to overcome "the domination of nurses as women by medicine, health agency administrators, insurance leaders and legislators (mostly men)," she wrote. "Yet large numbers of nurses appear willing to transfer the determination of their employment and professional rights to still another type of male domination—the labor union. How ludicrous and self defeating! Do we really have to have 'big daddy' do it for us?"

Many union nurses felt more affection for their industrial counterparts but still strongly favored a discrete nurses' union. There were, after all, life-or-death issues on the bargaining table. They needed representatives who understood the medical and interpersonal dimensions of the job. Diane Goddeerian often uses the figure of "seven minutes" to illustrate how long a caregiver might have to intervene after a traumatic event before a patient faces irreparable changes. Can you get to the bedside? Can you get a doctor? Can you get the ancillary staff and equipment necessary to intervene? Are you disoriented at the end of a mandated double shift? Someone's life course is at stake, Goddeerian says, and "there's no turning back if the seven minutes go by and you weren't there to take care of them."

———————

Soon, nurses saw the gulf widen between their values and those of an increasingly commodified healthcare system. The Reagan administration spurned the era of regulatory cost-containment, instead imposing price mechanisms to allow market competition to structure the healthcare industry. This led to economic polarization in the healthcare industry, forcing many community hospitals to merge or shutter while prestigious hospitals continued to expand, and setting the stage for healthcare conglomerates to grow and consolidate. One of the most significant changes was the prospective payment system, a 1983 insurance reform that further incentivized hospitals to direct money towards high-intensity illness care and away from any sort of care that wasn't illness-treatment—like the comprehensive care that nurses provided.

Even as hospitals needed nurses to achieve outcomes they could be reimbursed for, they increasingly viewed nurses as a cost, rather than a source of revenue. The structure of Medicare and Medicaid did little to contradict this view. MNA nurses complained in a 1984 statement that third party reimbursement policy hindered "the demonstration of the cost effectiveness of nurses in providing health care," partly because its paper trails attributed outcomes of nursing care not to the nurse, but to the supervising physician. Hospitals have still collected little data, or don't really want the data, about what revenue nurses generate, says historian Julie Fairman. Time and time again, this omission has justified minimizing costs in all aspects of nursing, from staffing levels to educational opportunities to wages.

The rallying cry for fair wages among nurses in the 1980s was the idea of "comparable worth": that workers were undervalued in industries where traditional "women's work" predominated. Today's correlative, the "wage gap," conjures images of managers covertly paying women less than men in the same roles. "Comparable worth" had a slightly different orientation, emphasizing how certain kinds of labor were treated or mistreated in the capitalist labor market. "The wage and salary concerns of all women are embodied in the wage and salary concerns of nurses," wrote Furlong in 1984. "No other female occupation provides such a glaring example of the failure of market forces to determine appropriate wage rates."

That hospitals continually wrote off nurses as a line cost, or even as part of "the room charge," as one Michigan nurse put it, demonstrates the same effect: how labor deemed "women's work"—whether or not performed by women—is systematically devalued because it is viewed, like housework, as the backdrop that sustains productive activities, and not a productive activity in and of itself.

Facing an increasingly medicalized healthcare landscape, the "professional" label took on a new weight. It seemed like a way to possibly, finally, define nurses' labor—not only for the sake of recognition, but to make it visible on the hospital's revenue statement.

"Nurses have had a hard time establishing their professional identity because medicine is based on outcomes, and it's hard to quantify outcomes from nursing practice, although there are clearly outcomes from nursing practice," says Anne Jackson, who started her nursing career at the university in the mid-'80s. As an ambulatory care nurse, she explains, hospitals would like to quantify her by the number of phone calls she makes. But caring labor, no matter how expert, is existentially hard to define.

"Yes. You give the medicines. Yes. You take the vital signs. Yes. You monitor the patients," says Jackson. But really, the nurse "is kind of like a MacGyver. Here is your patient with this problem. I'm not going to say what medicines they need. But they've got to figure out how to deal with this disease in their life. And it's the nurse that helps them figure out how to do that. What is your socioeconomic status? What is your education status? What is your health literacy?"

Jackson recently asked a pediatric patient what she was doing in the hospital. The girl's father was angry at the question, which was, in his view, needless. The doctor had already come in and diagnosed the problem.

"*I* knew why she was there," says Jackson. "I wanted to know what *she* knew. And so I was just sort of using the Socratic method to figure out what she knew, how she understood, what information I still needed to give her, without being rude and just blabbing at her."

In 2017, the "University of Michigan Health System" became "Michigan Medicine." To Jackson and many other nurses, the name change signified the culmination of a long arc towards commodified medicine, "making us completely medicine-driven, as opposed to a much more collaborative institution," she says. It felt like evidence that their contribution was no longer valued at the institutional level.

—————————————

In 1989, Deborah Stoll, a young intensive care nurse, walked to the UMPNC offices in Ann Arbor, near the hospital. She wanted to talk to Margo Baron, the union's chairperson. Stoll had struck in 1981, but had not known the ins and outs of bargaining. She was a young nurse, "showing up for work and having a good time and dating and putting money in my bank account."

Baron was busy preparing for the UMPNC's second work stoppage. The hospital was short-staffed and "stuffed to the gills," one node in a nationwide nursing shortage. Stoll remembers receiving notes from admissions: "Fifty-some patients admitted today and we have four open beds. Have a good day!"

Managers used mandatory overtime to respond to the shortage, forcing nurses, many of whom were responsible for children at home, to stay on without warning. Shifts were rearranged at will, from night to day or day to night, so workers could not plan patient care in advance, and sometimes found themselves working back-to-back shifts of up to twelve hours each, too tired to think straight. "Most everybody learned not to answer their phone because that could be their nurse manager on the phone telling them they had to come in on their day off," says Stoll. "Everybody bought answering machines."

Nurses reported a cycle of exhaustion, stress, and unsafe care. "A lot of it was the same issues that we're having now with short staffing," says Jackson.

Stoll asked Baron if she could help with anything, and Baron had her call nearby hospitals to send nurses to work in the event of a strike. Stoll became wrapped up in the collective bargaining process. Her knowledge grew. Her attachment to Baron grew: "I think, somewhere in the back of her mind, she chose me as her predecessor without telling me that."

This time, eighty percent of the university's RNs walked out. They demanded that management end mandatory overtime and staff the hospital floor at levels appropriate for safe patient care. By striking explicitly over staffing, nurses had found a locus for their concerns as workers and caregivers. The demand for staffing ratios explicitly linked the interests of the worker to those of the "third person" in nursing labor negotiations—the patient.

Ultimately, the union won a large wage increase instead of improved staffing language. It was hard to say whether the money got to the heart of the matter; it temporarily raised staffing levels by attracting more nurses from around the region. Other hospitals across the state were forced to raise wages in response. The victory was meaningful, but ephemeral.

There was an agreement, for a few years, between employer and union, that two strikes in nine years had been too much, with no real victors. Together they tried something unusual in the field: they transitioned to "mutual gains," a less confrontational, more consensus-based approach to bargaining. Stoll had become a spokesperson during the strike. "And then Margo appointed me to continue on with the bargaining team after fact-finding," she says, "so I did that. And then she asked if I would run for chair, and I did that."

She was grateful that the shift to mutual gains coincided with her tenure as chair. She felt she could not survive the head-butting of big, traditional labor negotiations. "Compromise was part of my career, part of my internal core," she says. "But it is not easier, let me tell you. It is not easier at all. It's very time consuming and very difficult." For a few years, nurses and management collaborated to promote nursing autonomy and prevent the workload issues that had prompted the strike. But then, says Stoll, mutual gains "just became harder to do."

By the 1990s, the nature of healthcare labor was transformed. Healthcare systems began warring with insurance companies over rates. Hospitals responded to the pressure by "restructuring": a mass adoption of "lean models" of medicine and "just in time" policies, practices borrowed from industrial manufacturing to operate using the minimum amount of resources. Even wealthy university hospitals that had avoided the effects of a staffing crunch in the previous decade felt one now.

At the University of Michigan, as time dulled the acuteness of the strikes and administrators turned over, "it became harder to get the buy-in from management, who had things they wanted, and didn't really care why we didn't like them," says Stoll. "They were sliding back into a more traditional bargaining process, and I think they're firmly there right now." Nurses lost interest, too. "Sometimes you just want to get mad and get even, and mutual bargaining doesn't allow that."

Over the next decade, the ANA also became less sympathetic to labor. Its nurse manager leaders disliked the strong influence of traditional unions and aligned its priorities increasingly with hospital administrations. By 2008, its leadership proposed a change in its bylaws which would effectively disenfranchise its labor arm, the United American Nurses (UAN). In the past, member organizations had paid their dues to the ANA, and a large portion went towards labor representation. Under the proposed bylaws, dues would remain the same, but would no longer fund bargaining. The state organizations faced a financial ultimatum to choose between the century-old institution and the now severed labor arm.

The vote over the new bylaws was to take place at the ANA's annual meeting of state delegates in Washington D.C. in 2008. Michigan, one of the UAN's most active constituencies, was at the center of debate about the bylaws. The MNA's president, Cheryl Johnson, also headed the UAN. But the MNA's influence and morale took a sharp hit when Johnson died abruptly in October 2007. Her death left Diane Goddeerian, then a nurse at Sparrow Hospital in Lansing, to steer the state union.

In the months leading up to the vote and throughout the conference, UAN's core members tried to propose alternatives. They felt hospital systems would be more empowered to conquer a divided nurse workforce. But they felt the absence of Johnson's knowledge and leadership. Another disadvantage was that executive nurses were overrepresented in these conversations; because the conference was expensive and meant taking several days off work, most staff nurses could not attend. The Michigan nurses decided in advance to withdraw from the ANA if the delegates voted for the split. When it happened, they walked out of the conference and into the unknown.

I asked Goddeerian if she was there that day. "Now you just sent chills down my spine," she replied, "because yes. I had to get up to the microphone and announce that we were leaving. I remember one of the phrases in that speech was, 'ANA is a house with many rooms. But you've made it clear there is no room for the nurses in the labor union.' And we were done."

The choice to leave was divisive among nurses in Michigan. Friendships suffered. "It was hard to be in the middle because there was no middle," says Goddeerian. But a few other union states left the ANA soon after, and California and Massachusetts had both left a few years earlier, and they had survived. "You just had to say, for the greater good, for the nurse's voice to be heard in the workplace, we have to do this," Goddeerian says.

California nurses had also achieved something new: they had lobbied successfully for minimum staffing levels to be written into state law, like those that governed the airline industry. If staffing ratios were legislated, unions would not have to renegotiate them in contract after contract. The state unions that had left the ANA joined with California and Massachusetts to start a larger push in the political arena—"Something that nurses have never been very comfortable with," notes Goddeerian— to promote staffing bills at the state and federal levels.

This alliance became National Nurses United (NNU), today the largest nurses' union in the country with a membership of about 225,000. In its early days, NNU agreed to partner with the AFL-CIO, reflecting the new union's desire to cultivate broad solidarity and a voice in the national labor movement. There was a logic to the affiliation, Goddeerian says. After all, almost everyone in the AFL would spend some time in a hospital, and when they did, they would want to be safely cared for. Having them understand "our issues, understand what staffing ratios mean, it's very important," she says. "They might not have paid attention to it, because they're working on their issues. Well, then our issues become their issues, too."

At a hearing in the Michigan legislature over staffing legislation, Goddeerian remembers a committee member asking a nurse manager, who was representing the American Hospital Association, "Are there any staffing levels in the bill that you could agree to?" She said no, expressing the most common criticism from opponents of mandatory ratios: that nurses should use their professional judgment in the moment to act in the best interest of the patient. The two went back and forth. The committee member asked if the nurse manager could agree to a ratio of one nurse to one patient in the operating room, typically considered a common sense standard. She evaded the question: "Well, I think at the time we would look at that."

Goddeerian remembers thinking, "Can't you just do the right thing and say, 'Well, yes'? And it didn't come out."

———

To this day, no "safe staffing bill" has passed in Michigan. Nurse-to-patient ratio laws exist only in California and New York. In recent years, state affiliates of the contemporary ANA, now widely perceived as a managerial nurse organization, have joined with the American Hospital Association to campaign against versions of this bill.

In the pandemic, the consequences of short staffing became more dire as nurses reached new heights of stress, exhaustion, and "moral trauma" from tending to life-or-death situations under needless conditions of scarcity. The ANA's position on staffing has nonetheless become more ambiguous: on its website, it promotes "mandated nurse to patient ratios or standards," but it does not support an NNU-backed federal bill which would establish them. The NNU, meanwhile, has emerged as a giant in the labor landscape of the pandemic, bearing the torch of the staffing demands that first took shape in the 1980s.

Looking back at the past decade and a half from a historian's view, Fairman has noticed what she calls a "sea change" in nursing labor movement's rhetoric on staffing. It has grown less focused on caregiving and the need to be properly compensated for it. Instead, it tends to point to a large body of research, conducted since the 1990s, demonstrating the inverse relationship between staffing levels and patient mortality. Unions have drawn on this evidence to emphasize patient safety, the idea that "if you don't give us better working conditions, our patients are going to suffer," Fairman says.

It may be that partnering with other national unions has helped nurses strategically identify where their power lies, and thus, how to situate their demands. Emphasizing that "we care for you" has never served American nurses very well, Fairman says. "'Patient safety' is a less gendered term and actually gets more public recognition."

Nurses' political messaging has required the same principle of self-sacrifice as their old professional mandate. "It had to be more about the patients than about the nurses themselves," Fairman says.

The MNA's wins have become more frequent and more substantial. Lately, it has had the most success unionizing nurses in the Upper Peninsula, where most of the hospitals are relatively small. It is becoming more and more difficult to organize large corporate hospitals with money to pour into union-busting efforts. The long shadow of the profit-driven consolidation of the '80s and '90s stretches across Michigan. Two health facilities, Beaumont and Spectrum, merged this year: the resulting 22-hospital system dethroned both Ford and General Motors as the state's largest employer. Administrators have brought in consultants to cut $200 million per year. In some ways, the opposition facing healthcare unions is at its fiercest. But healthcare unions have risen to the occasion with equal intensity.

"Now is really a particular time, don't you think?" muses Fairman. As nurses leave the profession in record numbers because of the conditions of the pandemic, she believes hospitals and the public are at last beginning to understand nurses' value. They might just be able to change the course of healthcare if they are able to seize the moment as a collective. "Hospitals exist—and this should have been recognized so long ago—hospitals exist because people need nursing care. And nurses are really the linchpin of what happens in those institutions," she says. "So, this is nurses' time."

The Cost of Loss at WVU

RACHEL ROSOLINA

Appalachia has an extraction problem. From coal to timber to clean water—and now our brightest minds—the natural resources of this mountainous region have been snatched from beneath us, profits pooling instead in faraway cities. We have long endured an economy governed by outside corporations and distant landowners, where the bottom line is king and calculated costs are worth the incurred loss. Despite being in a state with a storied history of forfeiting resources, West Virginia University has decided to risk a brain drain in lieu of a long-term solution to its budget shortfall. As a WVU alum, I thought we knew better than to sweep our own riches out the door.

In a confusing case of self-sabotage, WVU recently released preliminary recommendations to address its $45-million deficit, which would discontinue 32 majors—12 undergraduate and 20 graduate—and 169 faculty positions. Losing the entire world languages program may simplify a spreadsheet, but it will also send talented West Virginians outside state lines for better opportunities. Cutting a bachelor's in recreation, parks, and tourism resources will close an obvious door on West Virginia's future economic opportunities. Discontinuing the MFA in Creative Writing program, of which I am a proud graduate, will limit promising writers from exploring and sharing the underrepresented Appalachian region.

According to their stated portfolio review process, WVU's shortsighted hack and slash approach centers on enrollment trends and whether a given area of study brings in research funding. This method highlights a profound misunderstanding of the importance of programs that don't bring in research dollars—many of which are in the humanities—and the cultural necessity of creative outlets. Beyond nurturing essential skills such as critical thinking, communication, and problem-solving, the humanities are a delayed investment that encourages stronger relationships and communities. The act of creating has long been an Appalachian cultural marker of resistance, allowing us to control our own narrative amid outsiders' labels, misrepresentation, and poverty porn. Consider Hazel Dickens's mournful protest songs, Appalshop's films documenting the aftermath of industrial accidents, and the many books celebrating the diversity of the region.

By ignoring root causes, WVU's actions will be no better than those of the many extractive companies that came before. Except perhaps that it is more painful to watch such a loss stem from within the state. Instead of following its mission to create "a diverse and inclusive culture that advances education, healthcare and prosperity for all by providing access and opportunity," WVU is pushing potential students away and limiting the very work that makes Appalachians resilient.

I know I've been lucky. Growing up homeschooled in the remote mountains of East Tennessee, I had no idea that creative writing was an educational option. I fell in love with regional literature at Berea College in Kentucky, but it wasn't until I stepped through the stately doors of Woodburn Hall on WVU's Morgantown campus that I fully understood my own power: here, words had gravitas. They were a tool to make sense of one's past, a path to invite others in. And perhaps most important to me, as I had chosen WVU due to its location, Appalachian words in particular were to be treasured.

An obvious argument for the continuation of programs like the MFA in Creative Writing—which I am most familiar with—is representation. In my coursework at WVU, I was handed book upon book by writers who not only celebrated this region but also showed it as it was, without shame. My professors taught work from around the world, while highlighting the artistry flowing from these mountains. We had guest lecturers like West Virginian Ann Pancake. In her essay "Tough," I experienced the impact of seeing myself in another writer's words. Many classmates also went on to write their own books, like Sarah Einstein's memoir *Mot* or Sarah Beth Childers's *Shake Terribly the Earth: Stories from an Appalachian Family*. It was alongside these fellow writers that I felt pride in relaying the beautiful complexity of our region rather than relying on the quaint small-town takes or misinformed backwoods narratives invented by outsiders.

A more complex argument for finding a route forward other than cutting programs, however, is a question of value. Just as we have seen what our land and health are worth to coal and timber barons, we must also ask what our voices are worth. From the arrival of industry, the diverse people of this region have been told we are not good enough, not smart enough, that our accents are too strong, that we are not worth investing in—that we are worth actively stealing from. Appalachian value has always been in line with the profit we can turn for someone else, and WVU has seemingly bought into that worldview.

Academia has been shifting, quietly, for many years. Concerns about the impending enrollment cliff are whispered in meetings from the highest ivory tower offices to the basement of the libraries. Tenure-track professorships have morphed into adjunct positions, forcing academics to be consistently underemployed, many requiring several jobs to make ends meet in our current economy—especially in expensive college towns.

WVU's approach to this industry-wide problem has been to gamble on expansions and enrollment goals not based in reality. At some point it realized that if it stayed on that path, the deficit could reach $75 million as soon as 2028. Unfortunately, in an attempt to quickly counteract these drawn-out mistakes, WVU is asking the wrong questions. It is tallying the ledger with neat lines and tidy columns, eliminating programs that may not bring in money but that do the important work of blurring lines, questioning authority, and making people feel. Blaming its financial shortfall on an enrollment cliff instead of a decade of poor decisions is a self-made escape route. It is, to put it in literary terms, an emperor making $800,000 a year with no clothes who is also looking forward to retirement.

Cuts like those proposed will have a domino effect. WVU is the largest university in West Virginia and the state's only R1 school. With these drastic edits, West Virginia high schoolers will have fewer in-state options, which will lead to an exodus of talent. Once gone, the hurdle to coming home is that much greater. Also, by cutting graduate programs, WVU will face a lack of graduate assistants to help teach the entry level courses that remain. During my tenure at WVU, I taught English 101 and worked as the graduate assistant for West Virginia University Press.

My MFA indirectly allowed me to shape freshmen worldviews, see firsthand how books are made, learn marketable skills, and kickstart my career in publishing.

So instead of looking at cold numbers, WVU's decision-makers should be questioning the cost of loss. What voices will they silence? How many West Virginians will be disadvantaged due to lack of opportunity?

Appalachia is a geographically and culturally distinct area marked by the cancerous effects of extractive capitalism, and West Virginia is the only state completely within its regional borders. But while our ancient mountains may be isolating, their intricate green folds force a closer relationship with the land, a stronger sense of community, and a higher level of resolve. Regardless of what resources or opportunities are taken from us, we will overcome, as we always do. I just wonder what it would be like if our own leaders stood with us for a change.

#BuffaloSyllabus: A Love Letter to Black Buffalo

ADRIA R. WALKER

J Coley, a PhD Candidate in the Sociology Department at the University of Buffalo, immediately took to Twitter following the murder of ten people by a white supremacist at a Jefferson Avenue Tops grocery store to say, "I'm sick because I shop at that supermarket. It's located in a lower-income Black neighborhood in Buffalo. This terrorist sought out Black people to kill. Literally came to the hood to kill us. And live-streamed it all." Their sentiment gained traction, eventually amassing over 21,000 retweets and almost 125,000 likes. People across the country, not just in Buffalo, wanted to do something, wanted to understand how a tragedy like this could happen.

From the tweet, Coley connected with Robert A. Mays, a clinical social worker who was born in Buffalo, as well another Buffalo-born historian named Tiana U. Wilson who studies Black women's intellectual history, and William Jamal Richardson, a sociology PhD candidate at Northwestern University and another native son of the city.

As a sociologist, Coley's research is focused on the East Side of Buffalo, where the shooting occurred, so they already had information about the history of the neighborhood and they were in community with residents there. Coley has published research on gentrification, race and class in Buffalo.

"We were all on Twitter reacting with a bunch of other scholars and activists, just talking about naming the antiBlackness that happened in Buffalo," Coley said.

On a national scale, Wilson said, people were confused and outraged about what happened—Why was this Tops targeted? Why this neighborhood? Why Buffalo?

"A lot of people were hungry for more knowledge about the Black community and Buffalo," Wilson said. "I was really appreciative for scholars like J, who came at the forefront of this really troubling and devastating time to be in."

For those people, Coley's early tweets—informed by their research in and involvement with the East Side—were invaluable. They allowed outsiders, Wilson said, who were only able to engage with the East Side through social media and the mainstream media, to have a better idea of the community. The tweets were also instrumental in countering mistaken narratives about the community that began to coalesce in the mass media and online immediately following the shooting.

Inspired by the Charleston Syllabus and the Ferguson Syllabus, both of which were crowdsourced, social-media driven syllabi created in response to racist violence, , Coley tweeted out a call about creating a similar syllabus for Buffalo. Wilson, Mays and Richardson answered the call, and thus, on May 18, the Black Buffalo Syllabus Collective was born.

Over the course of about three months, Coley, Wilson, Richardson and Mays met, gathering resources and readings that they thought would be the most beneficial for the syllabus. Eventually, they decided to expand the wellspring of information by starting a social media campaign in which they used the hashtag "#BuffaloSyllabus." People on social media sites, primarily Twitter, then used the hashtag to share their resources, media, articles and research. The campaign lasted for about a month.

This online collective generated a Google Doc in which they collected all of the references and citations they received. From there, they selected the sources that they thought best fit the syllabus. Using those selected sources, the collective created the "official, official Buffalo syllabus," Coley said, which is housed at buffalosyllabus.com., which has been available to the public since September 15, just four months after the massacre.

A resource for everyone

Despite being created primarily by academics and their networks, you don't have to be an academic or scholar to use the site. Accessibility was crucial, and central, to the development of this resource. Endeavoring to ensure that the syllabus is accessible to everyone, the collective included podcasts, videos and short essays to make sure that the widest possible audience could engage with the materials in whatever capacity possible.

"It's really important to us—we would say we're all activist scholars—to make sure that our research is accessible to the public, especially because the Buffalo Syllabus was born out of our love for Black Buffalo and Black people," Coley said. "It's really important that we're making it accessible for folks that are outside of the academy."

Despite its rich history, culture and significance, Buffalo is "often lost in the narrative of New York City," Mays said. He explained that Buffalo is "lost in the narrative of the Great Migration," whereas cities like Chicago and Detroit maintain a prominent place in the popular imagination as destinations in Black migratory histories during the last century.

"It can be forgotten, and it can get forgotten that Buffalo has had a very sizeable Black population and a very prominent Black population that has produced a variety of different people—whether it's from athletes to singers to activists to people to community; and it's a thriving, living, breathing entity," Mays said. "It's not dead, it's not standing on one leg. It's actually a living, viable, breathing community with power."

The Buffalo Syllabus, then, exists not only as a love letter to Black Buffalo, but as a remembrance and acknowledgement. It serves to fill in gaps and correct narratives.

"That was the role (of the Buffalo Syllabus), … to unite and illuminate in a different way," Mays said. "Me, Tianna and Will are natives. We know our home. J lives home. To be able to do that was really a love letter, in a sense, to reground our work. I say 'reground,' but to maintain the groundedness of our works, our different works, and the love of home."

Wilson agreed, saying that "We really wanted to use the resources that we had in the ivory tower… to make sure that we're using the platform that we have to elevate the lived experiences of Black people in Buffalo, to demonstrate their historical and contemporary struggles that are rooted, that have a history of marginalization, segregation and discrimination—but also so much more." The syllabus, Wilson explained, exists as a way to intervene in what the scholars saw as the narrative around Buffalo that was perpetuated following the shooting.

"It was centered so much on this white supremacist person," she said. "His networks and what this means and connecting it to white supremacy globally and all of these things. But missing from that discussion was: how can this community begin to heal form the harm that was caused to them?"

In the weeks following the massacre, Buffalo lost its place in the news cycle. People moved on. But East Siders' lives have been forever changed.

"This is really a love letter to Black Buffalo," Coley said. "And we don't want to forget the ten people that were lost and the people that were traumatized. We're really hoping that Buffalo, Black Buffalo and even Black folks outside of Buffalo continue to receive the syllabus as such."

By creating and maintaining the Buffalo Syllabus, the collective hopes to help bridge the gap between the ivory tower and the community. This is reflected in the documents chosen for the syllabus. Instead of focusing solely on sources written by academics—though the syllabus does certainly include those—non-academic sources, including articles that aren't behind paywalls, YouTube channels and multi-media offerings are also included in the syllabus.

From "Readings on Racism, Violence, and Police Brutality in Buffalo," which includes articles like "Police misconduct costing Buffalo millions," to specific op-eds about the mass shooting, like "American Racism and the Buffalo Shooting," to "Reading on the City's Geography" which details Buffalo's spatial racial history, the Syllabus aims to be conclusive, while also being a living document.

The collective was also considered who exactly they anticipated their audience would be even as they were composing the syllabus. In short, they decided that it would be accessible and for everyone.

"This will be for white people, to teach them about race, teach them about Black Buffalo and marginalizations… This will be for the Black community, for them to know the legacy, the radical tradition that is left in Buffalo that they can build upon," Wilson said. "(It is) a teachable, living, breathing document that continues to change."

'An all-in-one stop document'

The collective anticipates the syllabus existing in perpetuity as a resource for people to discover and rediscover, to learn from and remember throughout the years. The collective hopes that people happen upon and learn from the syllabus for years to come, even as the national media has lost interest in the tragedy which occurred here.

"As time goes on, unfortunately this won't be the only terrorist attack in the Black community," Mays said. "Unfortunately, terrorism has been a natural part of Black lived experience across the Black diaspora, so this will be, unfortunately, one of many. But I hope that as other people use their voice, center their voice, ground their voice, that… this will impact one person. One person. We always focus on a thousand people, two thousand, a million—but we negate and neglect how important the one is."

Coley says the syllabus is already being used by some teachers in the Buffalo Public Schools District. The collective hopes that more teachers and professors, community leaders, elected officials and law makers and regular, everyday people start and continue using it, as well. For Wilson, the educational aspects of the syllabus are personal. Wilson attended Buffalo Public Schools, and she says the local Black history she was taught was lacking.

"What the syllabus holds is a major resource for school teachers and educators and community organizers to now have a list of sources that they can draw on to incorporate these types of documents, these stories, these histories into the curriculum, so that it is educating the next generation and provoking larger conversations," she said.

In the year following the shooting, many East Side residents have said that they feel as if the promises made for change in the wake of the shooting have fallen short or not happened at all. Coley hopes the syllabus can be useful for impacting change.

"I know that not much has been offered to the residents most affected by this, residents in the Cold Springs and Fruit Belt neighborhoods," Coley said. "We're hoping that even in discussions of policies that come out of this attack, that maybe they're able to consult the syllabus. It's an all-in-one stop document, where we talk about every single thing. We're hoping that that can be beneficial."

Coley specifically said that they would like to see changes in policy and the implementation of programs like reparations for East Siders.

"We're hoping that having this resource available to folks will lead them to hopefully make the East Side a better area for people to be in, for people to actually have the resources that they need," they said.

'There's Still Work to be Done'

Though there is some overlap, each member of the collective focused on different sections of the syllabus. Wilson, for instance, is drawn to the section that considers an abolitionist future. For her, that section provides readers with an opportunity to "think about alternative forms of healing that don't center the police or the carceral state."

"By uplifting community activists, their labor, their networks and their way to care for each other when all of this attention is gone—I hope models for the younger generation that more police are not the answer," Wilson said. "When you're focusing on the aftermath of this really tragic event, centering what the community needs… I think #BuffaloSyllabus offers a framework and a starting point to begin to have these types of conversations."

Coley thinks the history of segregation in Buffalo—a history that made it easy for the Tops shooter to find victims—is a good starting point for readers. Segregation in Buffalo, they said, is by design.

"It's not that Black people just chose that they all wanted to live in the same area," the said. "We know that through redlining and disinvestment and all these federal policies and state sanctioned policies and city sanctioned policies—that's what they wanted. They wanted the folks that were west of Main Street to have access to loans and to become homeowners. And folks that were east of Main Street, which is predominantly Black people, to not have access to loans to be able to get homes."

In the syllabus' section about segregation, the collective included texts and media that explore redlining and the exclusionary zoning of urban renewal that "displaced thousands of Black people and destroyed beautiful thriving communities," Coley said.

"We're giving you this history of all the things that led up to this Tops supermarket on the East Side of Buffalo being the ideal site for a white supremacist to enact an anti-Black terrorist attack," they said. "It's important to provide the history of Buffalo and saying that Buffalo is not that different from all of these other cities, all these other cities that are considered Rust Belt cities that had a lot of Black people migrate during the Great Migration. Buffalo is like a lot of these other cities, so if it could happen to Buffalo, it could probably happen—definitely happen somewhere else."

Drawing the connection between the history of racist policies and the legacies of those policies is vital, Mays said. It's not enough to know things happened and to view the past as having existed in a vacuum.

Racist policies, histories and decisions, he said, shaped the world we live in today.

"It impacts your housing, it impacts your health, it impacts your mental health, it impacts where you go to school, it impacts where you can buy a house (and) where you can't buy a house, it impacts your food, it impacts your built environment," he said. "The attack on that grocery store shut the grocery store down for months. That was an environmental injustice issue. So, the (section explains) that in a detailed way and really brings light to the lack of food options, grocery stores, supermarkets for people to shop for food is intentional… the separation is intentional, so is the subsequent response to that separation… Now you don't have access and you are cut off."

Mays notes that the racist and classist policies have not only harmed East Siders, but it effects other Buffalonians as well. The city of Buffalo is largely a food desert. Most grocery stores are on the periphery of the city or in the suburbs, but rarely in the city itself. Many of the stores within the city lack fresh produce and largely carry pre-packaged items. The built environment is "limiting and impacting people's physical health," Wilson said.

One of the aspects of the syllabus that is most important to Wilson is the way in which it highlights Black resistance. Growing up in Buffalo, she did not learn about the ways in which Black people resisted violence. The syllabus exists, then, in part, to fill in the gaps of what is provided in mainstream education.

"So much of the media is dominated by the violences that happened on these people, but missing from that is the agencies of these people and the work that community organizers and Black led institutions, the role that they played in resisting this violence," she said. "The syllabus offers that component as well, so I hope that future generations really find inspiration and a model for how to move forward."

The collective is aware of the number of sources they included— about 200 sources divided across twelve categories—and they know that people might be overwhelmed by the wellspring. But they see the syllabus as a beginning, not as a final destination or completed resource. In aggregating sources for the syllabus, the collective found a dearth of information about the Black experience in Western New York and about queer history.

"There's still work to be done," Wilson said. "I hope that more work continues to come out of this… More history on Black people during the Black power and the Civil Rights Movement. Black people, Black Buffalo and the abolition of slavery, that's still missing. Even in the midst of this long list, what was very revealing is the work that still needs to be done, which is exciting for young scholars, young educators, young activists (who are) interested in continuing to use education, political education as a tool to disrupt and challenge global white supremacy."

Erasure in Peoria

TAYLOR MICHAEL

A decade ago, Alexander Martin moved to Peoria, Illinois, from their mountainous West Virginia hometown, because "the vibes were right." The mid-sized, midwestern city in America's heartland was affordable, especially for an artist. Even on a fixed income, the multidisciplinary visual artist, drag performer, and adjunct professor of art history and studio art at Bradley University could create, live, and have fun. So, they laid down roots, creating their community, co-founding a nonprofit to support Black artists, and developing an artist residence for historically marginalized artists. Martin has not regretted the choice. While living and working in Peoria, they've enjoyed watching others start businesses, community organizations, and collectives to "make things happen" in the city known for containing the most average Americans. And so, at the end of summer 2021, they readily agreed to participate in a marketing campaign to encourage more people to move to Peoria. Martin enthusiastically agreed to tout their love of Peoria, but was shocked when even after the success of the campaign, they learned that some folks weren't on board with the kind of "mainstream American" Martin represents.

Discover Peoria, which is the Area Convention and Visitor's Bureau, commissioned McDaniels Marketing to film three videos profiling artists in the area who have been able to find work, develop friendships, and discover fun things to do in the city. Uploaded in September 2021, Martin's video includes clips of the artist at work in their studio, performing as a Drag artist under the name Artemisia VanHo, and interviews where they describe why they prefer Peoria over a larger city.

"There's so many people who are trying to better the community and provide resources for those who live and work in the area, and I wasn't expecting that," said Martin in the video.

Peoria County, which includes the communities of not only Peoria, but also Dunlap, West Peoria, and Mapleton, has always been a politically liberal county surrounded by far-more conservative central Illinois. Both in the recent presidential election and the 2020 midterm, just over 50% of voters selected the Democratic candidate. However, in the last decade, the area has become known as an affordable haven for LGBTQ+ people, which has increased a perceived difference with the surrounding rural areas. Recent statewide legislation in Illinois, protecting the right to an abortion, barring discrimination based on gender identity or sexual orientation, and securing trans-inclusive healthcare, made the state a highly favorable place to live, according to independent think tank the Movement Advancement Project. The LGBTQ+ advocacy group Human Rights Campaign's Municipal Equality Index scored Peoria slightly higher than the average United States city. Progressive policies combined with affordability make the county and city an ideal location for progressive and historically marginalized artists like Martin.

"Peoria is a pretty safe place for LGBTQ folks to live, work and play because there is such a vast network of everything from social activities to awareness events," said Nicole Morrow, the treasurer for the LGBTQ+ advocacy organization Peoria Proud. For example, Lit. on Fire, a woman, disabled, and LGBTQ+-owned independent new and used bookstore, opened in 2015 and has become a hub for community meetings. Owner Jessica Stephenson regularly hosts or promotes events with Jolt Harm Reduction Center, a nonprofit yoga studio, and Peorians for Reproductive Healthcare. Artemisia VanHo, Martin's name while performing in drag, often hosts story hours for children, sometimes partnering with Peoria Proud.

Despite being a haven for LGBTQ+ people, Peoria has long suffered an unrelated economic decline. The construction and mining equipment company Caterpillar Inc. moved its headquarters from Peoria to Chicago in 2017, costing the city jobs and residents. However, the decrease in property values created an opportunity for some looking for a more affordable city. Throughout the COVID-19 pandemic Tik Tok content creator Angie Ostaszewski, a friend of Martin's, has influenced an estimated 300 people from around the country to move to Peoria, highlighting the area's politics and affordability. Since the COVID-19 pandemic and 2020's George Floyd protests, residents and transplants have invested more in the city, forming more organizations and groups to help new and marginalized residents access resources, Martin said, adding that the "arts communities are trying to cross-pollinate, collaborate more, and support each other's events."

Some of the activities which make Martin such an important contribution to the community include their assistance in founding the Peoria Guild of Black Artists (PGOBA), an organization established in 2020 to uplift and support Black artists in the city, and that has partnered with Ameren Illinois Energy Efficiency Program since 2021, hosting a fall block party. In February 2022, the Illinois sustainable energy company partnered again with PGOBA, funding three murals, one of which Martin designed, relating to sustainability and community life. While Martin doesn't explicitly list any of these initiatives and policies by name in the campaign, they speak exuberantly about Peoria as welcoming and full of opportunity for folks looking to change their community. And it resonated with viewers. The film crew told Martin that the video had high engagement numbers in the first few weeks after its premiere. To date, on Discover Peoria's Facebook, the ad is the most popular video uploaded.

Therefore, Martin was confused when they heard from the marketing company at the end of 2021 that their video was no longer available on Discover Peoria's YouTube and website. Thinking the removal was an error, Martin did not follow up on the matter as McDaniels worked to fix the issue. But, in March 2023, they heard again the video still was not on YouTube or the website. This time, a friend working in Discover Peoria informed Martin that the video had made a board member or director uncomfortable and therefore was removed.

"And that was the nail in the coffin," Martin said. Despite assurances otherwise, they understood the removal to be an act of erasure, not a simple mistake.

Martin did not like the optics. Discover Peoria had *only* removed the video featuring a Black trans artist. Especially now, as state and local governments pass legislation policing Drag performers, limiting trans-inclusive healthcare, and banning books written by marginalized authors, this mistake should not be dismissed as a technical or administrative error.

"Especially in this current political climate, you censored a Black and trans voice," Martin said. "I don't care about the video going back up; I want you all to do better."

Within two days of Martin posting about the matter on social media to their nearly 2,000 Instagram and over 2,600 Facebook followers, Martin received a call from Discover Peoria executive director JD Dalfonso, who told the artist that the office wanted to resolve the matter. Dalfonso confirmed that Martin received payment, reassured them that the video would be reuploaded soon, and expressed that Discover Peoria did not have ill intent with that previous decision to remove the video. Martin elaborated that the video was not the only issue. They didn't need the exposure. Martin has received recognition for their work as an artist and advocate in a 2022 PBS Short Film Festival documentary. In 2020 *Peoria Magazine* named Martin a 40 Leaders Under 40 honoree.

In the conversation and a follow-up email, Martin asked for a public acknowledgment and apology. Whether or not the actions were purposeful or not, Martin maintained that the incident could cause harm. They wanted the tourism board to assure LGBTQ+ and Black residents that regardless of intent, the video's abrupt removal in the current political climate was irresponsible, and that Discover Peoria supported marginalized communities.

Discover Peoria's follow-up statement said the organization did not tolerate direct or indirect discrimination and expressed concern about the "speculated homophobic allegations." The nonprofit blamed the video's disappearance on a change in marketing strategy and offered links to the Facebook post and their website's media gallery (the media gallery link is no longer active, and the video is not available to the public on the website.) Martin found the response frustrating. The emailed letter did not address their specific concerns or seek to amend the situation.

From there, Martin worked to draft a petition and letter they presented to the Peoria City Council on April 25, 2023. Discover Peoria's revenue comes primarily from local tax revenue. Martin thought residents should have a say if the organization misrepresented or censored residents whose tax dollars fund the nonprofit tourism board's budget. At the meeting, Martin called for a public apology, an official audit of Discover Peoria's content, and a plan to better represent the city's diversity or risk losing their tax-generated funding. The petition amassed over 550 signatures, over half of those coming from current and former Peoria residents, business owners, and artists.

"I would like an apology to the community, acknowledging that [Discover Peoria] supports and uplifts all voices in the community, not just a specific demographic, not just a specific area code," Martin said at the City Council Meeting.

An informal audit Martin performed of Discover Peoria's social media, blog, and video content found more coverage of St. Patrick's Day, golf courses, and archival photos than cultural events, Black or Women's history month posts, and LGBTQ+ related events. And blog and social media posts seemed to feature cities in the metropolitan area, like Dunlap or Morton, which are predominately white, wealthy, and conservative, over Peoria. Martin hopes an official audit will improve transparency about how the city is marketed compared to the surrounding suburbs.

But lack of inclusion for marginalized communities is not a new issue in Peoria. Despite Black people accounting for over 25% of the population, over 40% of Black families live at or below the poverty line, according to 2023 data from the City and Peoria County Joint Commission on Racial Justice and Equity. In 2019, *Governing Magazine* published a series investigating racial segregation in central Illinois. Reporters found Peoria had the sixth highest level of segregation of any metro area, and the schools were the most segregated in the country, beating out cities like Boston, Detroit, or Little Rock, which have had historic battles over federally-mandated school integration. Before the 1968 Fair Housing Act, zoning regulations allowed developers to keep "undesirable" affordable housing units, which primarily housed Black families, far from residential neighborhoods with better school districts and a higher percentage of white families. Discriminatory lending practices barred many Black families from taking out mortgages and loans to leave or renovate their communities.

Concerns over property values have continued to keep Peoria segregated. When the Peoria Housing Authority released their plans to build a thirty-unit building in a northern, predominately-white part of the city to community feedback in March 2014, most residents rejected the plan. They worried about an increase in traffic, noise, and crime and a decrease in property values. A similar project in another predominately white neighborhood met equally fervent pushback because residents were worried about overcrowding children in the Dunlap school system.

This racial divide among Peorians seems reflected in Discover Peoria's content choices, according to freelance graphic designer and PGOBA member Morgan Mullen. She agrees with Martin that the image of

Peoria that Discover Peoria presents often excludes Black and LGBTQ+ communities in favor of the white, affluent suburbs. It's why Mullen signed the petition. Discover Peoria's decision to remove Martin's video was a "slap in the face" to Mullen. The move sends a message that it's okay to work in Peoria, but that people should invest in the predominantly white communities outside the city center instead. Even with Discover Peoria publishing pages to promote Black-owned or Hispanic-owned businesses, she adds that there was no substantive community outreach.

Nicole Morrow, who signed Martin's petition, echoes the belief that partnerships between local organizations, such as Peoria Proud and Discover Peoria, would be a step toward resolution. She suggested that the partnership could resemble Peoria Proud's relationship with the Peoria Chamber of Commerce. Over time, the two entities have built a relationship with trust and mutual respect to ensure resources reach LGBTQ+ business owners and residents.

Speaking about their relationship with the Chamber of Commerce, Morrow said that "We're adding LGBTQ businesses to the chamber so that they can benefit from all of those things a chamber membership provides and asking how do you make your boards diverse, make sure your staff are trained to handle issues and support diversity and inclusion efforts."

She notes that cultivating a diverse staff and board of directors would help combat the conservative mindset, which pressures employees to remove a video when a board member becomes "uncomfortable."

Jessica Stephenson agrees with this sentiment, saying that letting the issue go is dangerous in the current political climate. "If we let this slide, then we are sending a message that we are okay with Black and trans voices being silenced in a world that is already rife with that behavior," said Stephenson.

As of this article's publishing, the video is live on YouTube but unlisted, so not available through search and on Discover Peoria's channel homepage. The video is also still unavailable on the website. Discover Peoria has not responded to a request for comment. McDaniels Marketing has not responded to a request to comment.

In Pittsburgh, Local Journalism is Worth the Fight

NOELLE MATEER

Local journalism is the best journalism, and I know this because I've seen its opposite.

I grew up in Pennsylvania, went to college in Pennsylvania, and wrote my first stories in Pennsylvania—and yet I began my journalism career in Beijing, China. This was never the plan. If it had been, I might have considered learning Chinese. In college, I had vague ideas about doing a year abroad after graduation, but those ideas turned into concrete plans only after I surveyed the grisly job market that awaited me upon my release from school. Internships in places like New York and Washington, D.C. were largely unpaid; entry-level jobs were only marginally better. My advisor tipped me off about an internship in Beijing that offered housing and a stipend. I didn't know anything about Beijing. I ended up staying six years.

Ever since I moved back to Pennsylvania, I've been thinking about how that weird, life-altering chapter—the formative chunk of time I now just call "my twenties"—was the result of mostly boring economic factors. Sometimes I wonder, if the job situation had been tipped in another direction even a tiny bit—say if I graduated *before* the recession, instead of after it—would I be an entirely different person now? Would I live in a fancy coastal city? Could I have even avoided hassle entirely, and stayed in Pennsylvania? Because the irony of all this international job-seeking is that I eventually found the most fulfilling job of my life in Pittsburgh, Pennsylvania. And the irony on top of *that* irony is that three months after I started, my colleagues and I at the *Pittsburgh Post-Gazette* went on strike.

The reasons for our strike have been well documented elsewhere (read about them if you'd like). I'm not here to rehash our issues, but rather explain how rare and beautiful a place like the *Pittsburgh Post-Gazette* is, and why local journalism in places like the Rust Belt, even in its old-fashioned, traditional form, is worth fighting for.

Within a few months of landing in Beijing, I became aware that getting stories published would be relatively easy. News sites back home didn't want to spend their shrinking budgets on sending reporters abroad, but I was already abroad, in the country they increasingly wanted coverage of. I began stringing for a buzzy New York-based news company, and they ran pretty much whatever I sent them, twice a month. I still didn't speak Chinese, but I got to write and be published, all due to the happy accident of landing in a place that was considered important, news-wise.

I look back on some of those articles and cringe. They're not particularly insightful, and some even contain factual errors (the New York-Based News Company did not, apparently, employ fact checkers). Sometimes, now, I see the reverse of what I did—journalists from elsewhere coming to Pennsylvania and reducing it to cliches. But it took me a long time to make that connection.

I used those clips to get a full-time job, and then I began my slow ascent up the journalistic ladder. There was a pecking order in the international journalist set, with people like me at the bottom, and bureau chiefs for major news organizations at the top. I started as a writer for a small company, and then I became editor at the small company. Eventually I accumulated enough experience to apply for a better-paying job at a major international news corporation—one of the ones with a fancy bureau. I made it through a couple rounds of interviews, and then the Major International News Corporation said it was time for me to take a writing test.

At the time of the test, a hiring manager called to tell me there'd been a flood in Japan. She sent over a dossier that contained messy notes, weather reports and transcripts from eyewitnesses. I would have one hour to turn this into a story. Within that hour, I was also to rank a list of breaking-news headlines by order of importance. I would need to decide which is a bigger deal: the natural disaster in Japan, or the bombing in Sri Lanka? The political scandal in Myanmar, or the oil spill in the Philippines?

As I scrambled to cover the fictional flooding disaster for no money, just the hint of money in the future, I thought, *I've never been to Japan.*

I thought, *I'm a 26-year-old white girl*. And then I thought, *this is stupid*. The job's scope of coverage was "Asia"—an entire continent. A friend of mine had also just gotten a job for a different but similar Major International News Corporation, and he too covered Asia, only his bosses defined "Asia" as also including Australia and New Zealand. He was struggling with the fact that everywhere he went to report, he was a visitor—how could he be certain that what he was writing was good? If I took this job, I would be a constant visitor, too.

This is how I learned the paradox of the modern journalism career - the higher up the ladder you climb, the more you have a bird's eye view. That is, the more prestigious the role, the more the reporter is asked to see people as populations and not individuals; data points in stories about broad, sweeping trends. It's the opposite of what most of us start out doing in college journalism classes, hyperlocal stories on local car wrecks and lagging social services. Those "smaller" stories, which require us to interact with people in our own communities, in person, are the reason most of us fall in love with reporting. And yet, due to mostly boring economic factors—such as which media companies have the most resources and therefore prestige—the aspirational among us are encouraged to leave all that behind.

And when it comes places like the Rust Belt—in particular its more rural areas—the shrinking job market lures young journalists far from home. Over the past nine years, I've seen my classmates from journalism school bounce from one news market to another, going from small town to bigger town to small city to big city.

Eventually, I landed in Pittsburgh.

When I joined the staff of the *Pittsburgh Post-Gazette*, I encountered, for the first time, people who'd made lengthy, enriching careers out of news that was close to home. The journalistic ladder was different before the recession; they stayed in one place, and in journalism, thanks to the power of good union jobs. And that made their work better. My colleagues who've worked here for decades have roots in the communities they cover. They have deep expertise and long lists of sources. They can be sure that what they're writing is good because they're the ones most qualified to do so. And they get to do the best kind of journalism - local journalism.

Before we went on strike, I had some of the most fun I've had reporting in years and plans to do more. One afternoon, I met some local roboticists at a garage in the East End to strap on their new robot shoes and wheel around with tiny engines on my feet. I did an interview with a guy who steers a floating tiki bar up and down the Monongahela. I had plans to meet a group of Carnegie Mellon engineers at a slag heap where they test self-driving off-road vehicles (journalists who think local news is boring simply do not know what they're talking about). This is a misconception I've encountered repeatedly since going on strike - People assume you're striking because you hate your job. I'm striking because I love my job. I want to protect it.

Not every city our size has such a large and talented newsroom. And in the future, I fear even fewer cities will. The shrinking market has already devastated news sources in rural areas; it's coming for Pittsburgh, too. Organizing is a way of fending all this off, because without unions, the faulty decisions of media's wealthy owners go unchecked. Earlier this month, the owners of the *Post-Gazette*—who could end our strike by reinstating lapsed healthcare for production workers for measly tens of thousands—bought Pittsburgh's beloved alt-weekly, *Pittsburgh City Paper* (the purchase amount hasn't been disclosed, but I think it's safe to assume it was more than the cost to end the strike).

None of us are sure what this will mean for the two publications going forward. But having two major news sources in the city owned by notoriously anti-worker management can't be good. For local journalism to be good, local journalism *jobs* need to be good.

This has an impact beyond the workers who make newspapers happen. I've been thinking lately about my early-career freelancing luck, and how it boiled down to living somewhere considered newsworthy. Journalists clustering in national news hubs on the coasts has had the opposite effect for Pittsburgh; stories here only rarely make national news sites. The Major International News Company I once applied to wrote about the *New York Times'* one-day strike in December, calling it "historic." It has not covered the strike at Pittsburgh's largest newspaper at all—and we've been striking for three months.

We can't expect national news services to fill in the gaps left open by shrinking local news. When local journalists leave, news goes with them. My colleagues and I are striking because Pittsburgh deserves good journalism.

Your city deserves good journalism, too.

GEOGRAPHY & ENVIRONMENT

East Palestine: A Portrait

MATTHEW CHASNEY

Sulphur Run flows parallel to the Norfolk Southern railroad tracks on the eastern side of the village of East Palestine, Ohio. It dips under the tracks to the south side of the line where it cuts a course through a quiet, working-class neighborhood, then through downtown, on toward the city park where it merges with Leslie Run. From there it flows into the north fork of the Little Beaver River which is a tributary of the Ohio River.

When a Norfolk Southern freight train carrying hazardous materials, including vinyl chloride, derailed on February 3rd, the creek was a natural drainage basin for the toxic runoff that was released from the car. The subsequent vent and burn of the derailed cars made a massive smoke plume that was visible for miles.

The creek is the most enduring and visible evidence of the derailment. Weeks after the wreck the creek still smells intensely like chemicals despite the efforts of environmental remediation crews. Furthermore, the Ohio EPA collected thousands of dead fish from Sulphur Run and Leslie Run.

For the residents of East Palestine that live along its banks, they must contend with a stark question—stay and risk getting sicker or leave everything behind.

Gary Taylor and Tracy Wright live in a cozy home on Rebecca Street where the creek enters a culvert directly below their house. Gary is blind and Tracy has multiple sclerosis. Neither of them had family that could house them and their cats long term during the evacuation. Before the wreck Gary found a new job in Butler County, PA. They plan to leave as soon as they feasibly can.

Gary and Tracy's house on the culvert.

Environmental remediation crews working to clean Sulphur Run where it enters downtown.

Courtney Miller tosses a minnow trap into Sulphur Run. In three weeks of testing she hasn't turned up any living aquatic life. She bought her home on East Taggert Street four years ago and planned to turn it into a self-sufficient haven with chicken coops and gardens. It was heaven for her and her two children until February 3rd. Since the wreck she has been staying with a friend in Pittsburgh. Her kids have been living part time with their father in Chester, WV and commuting to her in Pittsburgh.

Since the spill, a video of Courtney showing an oily substance floating from the bottom of the creek has gone viral and she's made the rounds in the media. She has been suffering from sore throats, headaches, and difficulty breathing. She's angry and she intends to hold Norfolk Southern accountable. She plans to move permanently and leave everything if she has to. I asked what her next move is. "To breathe again," she replied.

Volunteers distributing bottled water to East Palestine residents on Market street.

Danny and Karen Bostwick purchased their vacation cottage along Sulphur Run instead of going on a honeymoon. They liked the idea of having a small town escape that was close to their home in Cleveland. Danny returned to the cottage and couldn't stay in it longer than fifteen minutes before feeling ill and leaving. The Bostwicks are weighing their options, but they accept that they too may have to leave.

Creek bed and water samples collected by the Bostwicks. East Palestine residents complain that the chemicals are settling on the creek bed and that the remediation efforts are ineffective.

Danny and Karen enjoy a fire in their backyard along the creek.

Saturday Afternoon at the Last Dog Track in America

ASHLEY STIMPSON

At around noon on an overcast Saturday in January, the clubhouse that overlooks the dog track at Wheeling Island Hotel and Casino is beginning to show signs of life. The TVs have all been flipped on, horses galloping across their tiny screens, while a yellow-haired women in a blue apron stocks bags of chips behind the concession stand. Meanwhile, spectators are starting to trickle in, racing programs folded under their arms. Lots of them have gray hair; nearly all of them are clad in a cotton/poly blend.

Eddie Walker is one of the early birds. A 66-year-old in a Ford hat and a flannel shirt, he's been coming to the track for nearly fifty years. His dad was partial to horses but took Eddie to watch he greyhounds run a couple times a month during his teenage years. When Eddie met his wife Cheryl back in 2004, their first date was at the movies—their second was at the dog track. Cheryl says she got hooked on the sport immediately. "I like that there's no human involvement, no jockeys," the 64-year-old says. "It's just the dogs out there, doing their thing."

Today, Eddie and Cheryl have driven two hours from their home in Columbus, Ohio, to enjoy one of their favorite pastimes—and to introduce it to a first timer, their grandson, Riley Trembley. As the 14-year-old studies today's program, he tells me he's making wagers based on stats, not coat colors or cute names. "I'm in it to win it," he says decisively, his cheeks still red from the cold.

It's not an ideal time to get into greyhound racing. In 2018, voters in Florida, for decades ground zero of the sport, passed an amendment to ban racing there after 2020, striking what many thought would be its death knell. Since then, tracks in Iowa, Alabama, and Texas have all shut down. With the closure of Arkansas' Southland track at the end of 2022, West Virginia is now home to the last two dog tracks in the

"

United States—the one here in Wheeling as well as Mardi Gras Casino and Resort outside of Charleston.

Yet even as tracks around the country flickered out, the West Virginia legislature has shown a convincing unwillingness to scrap the sport, which employs some 1,700 people in the state. On the first weekend of the year, I came to learn more about state of racing here—and to ascertain how long it can last.

It's 1pm when we stand for the national anthem. By now, the room is half-full of people gripping plastic cups of beer and saran-wrapped sandwiches. Behind the track, a barge pushes containers of coal up the Ohio River and a lone shaft of sun probes the skyline of Wheeling, like a spotlight searching for life.

By the time the men put their hats back on, Jill Spicer, a trainer at Xtreme Racing Kennel, has been awake for about ten hours. On race days, Spicer is up by 3am and in the kennel by 4:30. Once there, she turns out the dogs—she's up to 84 since inheriting 32 "new little recruits" from Arkansas' recently shuttered track—cleans beds, clips nails, pours breakfast, and weighs the hounds scheduled to race that day.

I greet Spicer when she pulls into the parking lot behind the paddock, quickly filling up with identical white dog trailers. As a cow-colored greyhound jumps out of one the truck's compartments, muzzled and twitchy with excitement, Spicer points to its purple leash and her purple sweatshirt. "We may not be the fastest kennel here, but we're the most coordinated," she hollers over to where I'm standing at the fence line.

From the parking lot, the trainers—each with anywhere from four to seven dogs in-hand—make their way inside the paddock for weigh-ins. Some of the dogs are here today for "schooling," practice races that demonstrate they're ready for the big leagues.

Between schooling and the 1pm post time, Spicer sits down in the clubhouse with me. She's wearing blue eyeliner and her thick hair in a braid. A couple tables over, a father tells his three sons to look at the camera. "First time at the dog track!" he announces as he snaps their photo.

At 56, Spicer has been in the greyhound industry for nearly forty years. She got her start at a track in Plainfield, Connecticut, where she spent summers working as a lead-out, walking the dogs from the paddock to the starting blocks before each race. Soon, she was working in the kennels, a job that took her to tracks in Alabama and all over South Florida.

The way Spicer describes it, life in a dog trainer is relentless. Thirty years ago, when she went into labor with her son Alex, she finished schooling the greyhounds before driving herself to the hospital. Three days later, she was back at the kennel, newborn in tow. "He has always had a dog beside him," she says. On holidays, the family "opened our presents after the dogs had gone to bed." And yet, Spicer insists working with the dogs is so fun, so rewarding, "it's not even a job."

But today, jobs like Spicer's are close to extinction. After the vote in the Florida— "something we never thought was going to happen," Spicer says—she was one of the lucky trainers who found work in West Virginia. Her son, now a trainer at a different kennel in Wheeling, was another.

"It's an honor to be able to race here," she says, "a real blessing." Spicer hasn't been here long, but she thinks the track is good for the Wheeling area, just as the track in her Connecticut hometown provided jobs and something to do on a Saturday afternoon. "Father, uncle, brother—everyone here has a connection," she says, pointing around the room. "It's nice to have a dog track in a small town."

Indeed, according to a 2014 West Virginia University study, greyhound racing in Ohio County contributed about $18 million to the local economy, generating approximately $214 thousand in county taxes.

If Spicer is worried racing could end in West Virginia anytime soon, she isn't letting on. Her grandson, who she pays five dollars a day to help out with the dogs, has already declared his intention to get into the family business. "The other day he said, 'Nana, I want to be a kennel owner,'" she tells me, positively beaming.

———————————

Wheeling Island transitioned from horseracing to dog racing and 1976 and there's one simple reason why it still exists here today.

In 2007, the state passed legislation law that said casinos could only offer table games and video lottery machines so long as they operated a dog or horse track. The Lottery Racetrack Table Games Act also established the West Virginia Greyhound Development Breeding Fund, which pulls about 1.5 percent of video lottery revenue (around $15 million each year) to subsidize kennel and breeding operations.

In the years since—as gaming revenue swelled and attendance at the dog racing withered—efforts have been made to decouple the two. The company that owns West Virginia's remaining tracks, Delaware North, is in favor of these efforts, telling West Virginia Public Broadcasting, "We would support it if legislation passed that would allow us to operate the casinos without operating racing."

In 2017, the legislature came close to doing just that, passing Senate Bill 437, which would have eliminated the Fund and allowed casinos to operate without live racing. But Governor Jim Justice vetoed it, saying in a statement, "If we get rid of greyhound racing it will mean job losses and fewer people coming to West Virginia. We can't turn our back on communities like Wheeling that benefit from dog racing."

Six years later, Chris Grieb, a trainer at McMillon Kennel in Cross Lanes, argues that West Virginia's monopoly on live racing should be considered an asset. "We have the only tracks in the country and people still like wagering," he says, "we'd be stupid to shut it down."

The people Grieb is referring to are mostly out-of-state betters, who wager their money online and via simulcast outlets, sitting in smoky casinos in Las Vegas, for example. On a Saturday afternoon like the one I spent in Wheeling, the handle—the total amount of money wagered on the dogs—typically exceeds a million dollars. It's a healthy number but only the track benefits from bets placed online or in casinos outside of West Virginia; the state does not collect tax on it.

Grieb arrived in West Virginia last summer, after the track he was working at in Iowa closed for good. The 52-year-old got a late start in the industry, when his first greyhound, a red dog named Sequoia, inspired him to get involved in the sport. In 2006, Grieb, a former high school football coach, moved from California to Florida to work in a kennel. Since then he's raised and raced dogs in Kansas, Arkansas, Iowa, and now West Virginia. "I have one of 25 jobs left in the country," he says about his role as a trainer.

Grieb admits there's a feeling he's come to the end of the line in West Virginia. While some of his colleagues are holding out hope for another decade of racing, he's banking only on another two or three. "Breeding is going way down," he says, "that makes things very difficult."

If racing ends, Grieb will miss the dogs the most. "I just love them so much," he says. "When you dedicate yourself to their wellbeing and see them come off the track after kicking ass, how much joy they have, that's what it's all about."

Back in Wheeling, by the time half of the day's twenty races are in the books, a flurry of losing bets litter the table that Matthew Rose and his friend Michael are sharing.

"We're running about even," Rose reports. The men, who work together at Akron's Northfield Park horse track, have been meaning to come bet on the dogs for months, and finally got a Saturday off. "It's relaxation for us."

"There's still a market out there for dog racing," Michael, who didn't want to share his last name, adds, "they're going to handle a lot of money today," he says, before heading to the cashier to spend some more of his.

A few tables down, Les Geiger taps a pencil against his program and fingers a stack of crisp dollar bills. The septuagenarian and his wife made the three-hour drive this morning from Springfield, Ohio. "The wife had some days off; thought we'd get away from the house." Geiger says he likes the track for the atmosphere—and the payouts. "I can't believe the prices they pay."

As we watched the 11th race of the afternoon—clinched by a yellow dog in the 8 jacket—Geiger tells me the casino hotel's 151 rooms were all booked for the weekend, so his wife, a hospital nurse, was taking a nap in the couple's truck. When racing is done for the day, they'll check into their hotel and have a nice dinner out, he says.

Proponents of racing point to visitors like the Geigers, Matthew and Michael, Eddie and Cheryl—people who wouldn't otherwise come spend their money in Wheeling—as compelling reasons to keep the sport around. But for every seat in this clubhouse that's taken, another one sits empty.

A Saturday afternoon at the dog track means spending a few hours at the surreal intersection of the past and future, where the air still holds memories of decades-old cigarettes and kids smile for a picture in a place they may not recognize a few years from now.

But none of that seems to bother Riley Trembley, who waves goodbye as he and his grandparents head toward the exit. The teenager proudly boasts that he won on four out of the ten races he bet on. When I ask if he'll be back, he doesn't say a word, just nods his head with an emphatic yes.

Fly-Fishing in Michigan

ED BREEN

It is neither broad nor deep nor of great length, this river. Just 64 miles of meandering, twisting and turning, flowing and gurgling through the forest and foliage of west Michigan. As the crow flies, only 30 miles from Baldwin to Ludington in the Lower Peninsula. But a creature of what beauty it is, this stream they call the Pere Marquette.

Pardon me today as we depart briefly from our Indiana neighborhood, board a small boat and float down a few of those miles of the Pere Marquette River in Lake County, Mich., mostly through the protected woodland of the Manistee National Forest.

This river, as with all rivers, has been here forever, or nearly so, carved by flowing water eons ago in the final days of the last great Ice Age, the same ice sheet that scoured northern Indiana and made of it a flat plain, shaving hills and filling valleys as far south as Monroe County today, making suitable space to grow corn and soybeans.

We don't know what this stream might have been named or how it might have been described by those first native people who undoubtedly waded these shallow waters, watching for fish darting this way or that, using primitive tools—spears, nets of woven grasses, early rods and hooks and carefully crafted weirs of stone – to snare and trap grayling and catfish and other creatures native to these waters long before more attractive game fish—notably a variety of trout and Pacific salmon— were introduced centuries later.

We know that this stream, like so many others to the far north of us, flows from the high ground down the sandy slopes of central Michigan, west toward the water of Lake Michigan. There are many similar streams: Au Sable, Manistee, Muskegon, Betsie, Leland, Boardman, and Baldwin. Michigan has more than 300 named rivers; by comparison, we Hoosiers have but 65.

We know that this stream was among the first to be given a European name. Its identification is with Father Jacques Marquette, the French-born Jesuit missionary and adventurer who died in 1675 at what is now Ludington, while exploring the Great Lakes shoreline. He was only 37 years old. The "Pere" in the name—Pere Marquette—is the Fresh translation of "Father," and it shows up on maps drawn in the 17th Century.

Then came the loggers who clear-cut the surrounding old growth pine forest and floated the millions—nay, billions—of board feet of timber down these streams to Lake Michigan, the logs ripping and tearing away the environment and natural banks of the rivers as they cascaded to the great lake. It was that timber that became the masts of sailing ships and the floors and ceilings of the homes and barns and factories that became the Midwest. And it was that timber that rebuilt the charred remains of Chicago after the Great Fire of 1871 and made it into the ration's Second City.

An aside here: Should you want to see what the primeval forestland was like before the lumbermen arrived, visit Hartwick Pines State Park just east of Graying, Mich., along I-75. Nearly 10,000 acres that can be described only as majestic. Red and white pines soaring 150 and 160 feet into the sky above the Midwest. Girth and circumferences of 10 and 12 and 13 feet.

Today, in easier times than those of the explorers on a religious mission and timber men in search of their fortunes, the Pere Marquette is spoken of in hushed tones by those who pursue fly-fishing for sport and amusement, rather than a necessary search for food.

Long expanses of the stream, departing from small places with names like "the bridge" and "clay banks" and "green cottage" are designated as catch-and-release waters; yes, you may catch the fish, but once you have been photographed proudly holding your trophy, you must release it unharmed back into its water world.

You may walk these waters in rubber boots and chest-waders, but if you prefer a boat, that's fine so long as there is no motor attached.

And you may snare the creatures here only on tiny hooks hidden inside artfully made "flies," handcrafted simulations of the bugs and insects that hatch on and over the stream, lead very short lives and are gobbled by the fish who erupt from the surface water to snatch dinner from the air.

Fly-fishermen—and especially those for whom the tying of their own flies is a religious ritual—are reverential people, like Presbyterians or Roman Catholics or Harvard grads. Fly-Fishermen.

The tying of flies is an off-season passion. Winters and time away from flowing water are devoted to this. They, these people, assemble great collections of tiny tools, like miniature surgical instruments, and assorted feathers and fabrics and tufts of hair and hide from horses and pheasants and other critters, which they sort and separate with tweezers. Their instructions, their guidance comes from the "recipe" for one or another fly. They have Bible-sized books of "recipes" on nearby shelves.

The object: To create feathers, fur and wire that imitate the look, flutter, wiggle and silhouette of a bug. A reliable source recounts from decades ago: The inveterate fly-tier was in need of a gob of gray fuzz. He found the color and texture in the living room carpet, took his scissors, trimmed the needed smidgen, returned to his desk and told his visitor: "Don't tell my wife."

And each fly bears a name. For this season and on this particular Michigan stream and under these weather conditions, there is the "Adam 14," and the "Sulphur 14." Then there is the "Gray Drake." They are what you and I would call May flies. Or a "PM Wiggle," a subsurface fly that wiggles when submerged in moving water. There is the "Bead Headed Nymph" and, of course, a Marabou, so named because it is fashioned from the marabou feathers found on the underside of a chicken's wing. There are hundreds—thousands!—more.

And there is evidence that fly-fishing—and all that accompanies it—is not restricted to the lonely and neurotic. An internet site enumerates current celebrities who fish with flies: Jimmy Buffet, Liam Neeson, Reba McEntire, Eric Clapton, Martha Stewart, Emma Watson, Harrison Ford. All are under suspicion.

There are terrible ironies here. Chief among them the reality that creatures with brains the size of a knuckle are able to consistently outwit, outsmart and outfox adults of the human species armed with thousands of dollars' worth of high-tech achievement: Monofilament translucent lines—they are called tippets—and rods crafted of split bamboo and, more recently, of graphite and resin, clothing made of Gor-tex waterproof textiles and one of everything in the Orvis Co. catalog.

No evidence that any living fish has ever made a purchase from an Orvis authorized dealer. But that's just me. Truth be told, I'm generally on the side of the fish in this titanic test. 'Tis true: I am not a fisherman. Not made in that factory, but I have always sought the companionship of those who were. They are, by and large, decent and enjoyable people with whom to associate.

In my misspent youth, it was pursuit of steelhead trout and salmon—King and Coho—on the Elberta Beach and Betsie River and the Two Hearted and other streams feeding Lake Michigan and Lake Superior. Cold gray skies, cold gray water. Twenty-something degrees and rain or ice spitting in from the west.

"Perfect," they said, these gap-toothed, slack-jawed, bow-legged, canvas-clad men who stored their day's catch in a second-hand ice cream freezer truck they drove north from a warmer place.

They understood that I was of little use to them. I sought only suicidal steelhead that hurled themselves on the beach, pleading to be taken to a smoker. But I was a pleasant storyteller in the evening hours and a reasonable drinker. Both desired qualities as steelheaders seek companions.

Satisfaction was accompanied by roaring fires built of driftwood on the beach and more warmth drawn occasionally from flasks tucked into snowmobile suits up and down the beach.

Today, in the declining years, I am among more affable folks in better weather and less demanding environment.

A log or tree stump or form-fitting boulder on the bank of this river, the Pere Marquette, will do nicely as we pursue this for the next thousand years or so.

St. Louis Brick by Brick

ANJULIE RAO

St. Louis is startling in its brickwork. Every home, it seems, is built from similar rust-colored bricks. Sometimes I wonder, just as you can see the lights of New York and Chicago from the International Space Station, if you'd also be able to make out St. Louis' distinct red-hue. Despite the material's ubiquity, each home is distinct; one residence might have raised thin brick defining the arched doorways, while the house next door uses inlayed patterns to decorate its roofline. Brick dentals, star-shaped bricks, swirled embossed brick—the pervasiveness of the material is matched by its variability, creating buildings as diverse as the bricks themselves.

Brick buildings have re-emerged in the architectural consciousness. In the Windy City, Brick of Chicago provides tours of remarkable and overlooked buildings which feature stone and terracotta; Tuskegee University architecture students studying their historic campus can examine the fingerprints from laborers pressed into clay bricks. In online architecture discussion, brick buildings conjure fantasies of *Times When Men Built Beautiful Things With Their Hands. "Why can't we,"* these posters ask, *"return to such simpler times?"*

New Orleans-based artist Jackie Sumell doesn't see the era of brick in such halcyon terms. Though her new project, *Freesoilparty*, an installation and performance series assembled for this year's COUNTERPUBLIC triennial of art and design in St. Louis (which closed this month), Sumell is telling a different rouge-colored story—the story of brick theft, the practice of illegally dismantling buildings and selling that iconic material to distributors who then provide said bricks to developers and architects outside of St. Louis. But her project goes beyond the bricks themselves: instead, she explores the material's connections to the region's history of displacement and extraction; a city that sits on stolen land is, again, being stolen. To understand the history of St. Louis's bricks is to unearth systems of power, economy, dispossession, decline, and manifest destiny;

the storybook decorative brickwork we see today becomes a tale as complex—and as sinister—as American history itself.

———————

For much of her two-decades-long artistic career, Sumell's work has addressed issues of incarceration and abolition. Having learned about the Angola 3 movement, she began corresponding with Herman Wallace, one of three Angola prisoners held in solitary confinement for decades. When their correspondence began in 2001, Wallace had been in prison for 29 of his 41-year sentence—most of it spent in solitary. Sumell and Wallace collaborated designing his "dream home" through letters over the course of their twelve years of friendship. The project, *The House that Herman Built*, resulted in a book, a documentary film, and a traveling exhibition that included visualizations and architectural details. Upon his death in 2013, Sumell found herself revisiting their letters and exchanges, and wanted to continue his legacy.

"I realized how much he talked about plants and gardening; he wanted the house made out of wood. When I first asked him what kind of house he wanted—a man who's lived in a six by nine cell—he said, *I can clearly see the gardens; they will be full of Gloxinia, delphiniums, and roses and I wish for guests to be able to smile and walk through gardens all year round.* So I knew there was meaning in gardening," she explains. Through gardens and botany, Sumell has found a "blueprint for human relationships," she says, as the natural world both represents and embodies liberation. Since then, much of her work has focused on plant life; notably, her project Solitary Gardens, where she constructed several 6'x9' garden beds—the same size as prison cells. The gardeners are incarcerated peoples in solitary confinement; they 'tend' to the gardens through written correspondence with liaisons.

The opportunity to contribute to COUNTERPUBLIC came from curator Risa Puleo, whose recent curatorial projects had also centered around issues of incarceration and its historical relationship to settler colonialism. COUNTERPUBLIC's 2023 theme, *Reclamations*, was an opportunity to stitch those larger themes together.

"There is something deeper that I'm not understanding about how the prison industrial complex and these questions about settler colonialism are entangled," she says. "I started inviting artists who were thinking about abolition or thinking about settler colonialism, but who are also working in these uncatchable mediums of plants and sounds as to offer us different kinds of ways of thinking through these problems."

What Sumell and Puleo found through their research on St. Louis was a deeply complicated, embedded history of removal and extraction—not dissimilar to Sumell's home in Louisiana.

"[Missouri and Louisiana] are deeply connected, not only through the Louisiana Purchase and colonization but through the Mississippi River. And so literally we are sharing the same water and the same soil," she says. Sumell happened upon an episode of the *99 Percent Invisible* podcast about the St. Louis "dollhouses," homes once occupied by Black St. Louis residents that had been "harvested" for their red, intricate bricks, and sold to developers downriver, "building affluence," she says, in new home construction under the guise of "reclaimed materials." But Sumell wasn't interested in reclaimed materials as part of the 2023 COUNTERPUBLIC *Reclamations* theme; instead, the bricks "harvested" from St. Louis speak to what, precisely, has been stolen.

Acknowledging that America was built in the stolen lands of native peoples, St. Louis, because of its strategic location along the Mississippi River and thus a hub for production and trade, has a particularly egregious history. *The Broken Heart of America: St. Louis and the violent history of the United States* by Walter Johnson (a book that Sumell notes she was asked to read prior to planning her COUNTERPUBLIC project), details how the city's history of extraction and colonization fueled its growth. Johnson writes of Meriwether Lewis and William Clark, who were chartered by Thomas Jefferson, to, "enumerate the Indians, announce to them the subordination of their nations to the United States of America, and gauge the economic potential of their lands." Missouri's "Indian Laws" of 1845 that banned indigenous peoples from living in the state, and prohibited trading with native peoples, stripping them of economic power.

The economic power St. Louis settlers grew throughout the nineteenth century, was made possible by such dispossession. One major economic engine became brickmaking. After a fire in 1849 that resulted in the loss of nearly $6.1 million of property, the city changed its building code to require that all structures be built from stone or brick, laying the groundwork for the city we see today. St. Louis, "got very lucky," says Michael Allen, president of the National Building Arts Center in Sauget, Illinois, just across the river from St. Louis. The city, he says, sits on the Cheltenham Syncline, a geologic formation that contains myriad unique deposits, most notably high-refractory red clay.

"It was mostly a materials convenience, because there's just so much red clay here," says Allen. The plentiful clay deposits led to mining the material within the city, producing open clay mines in places like Dogtown, an historically Irish community. Brickmaking blossomed with the invention of the hydraulic press in 1856, which mechanized the laborious manufacturing process and allowed the city's bricks to be sent westward as America expanded its territory through violent wars and further displacements of indigenous peoples, bringing to life the country's zeal for Manifest Destiny.

The brick was useful, says Allen, "where cities are being built out of nothing."

"In some ways, hydraulic presses, and maybe by association, red brick, is emblazoned in the history of St. Louis as this amazing capitalist commodity," says Allen. "Brick is one thing that we're selling to the rest of the country. And it can not only be used here, but we're one of the few places you could make this brick."

But brick continued to build St. Louis's residential and commercial footprint, accommodating a growing population that peaked in 1950. By then, racial covenants had been placed on 80% of the county's homes, making it a starkly segregated city. The buildings that are currently being dismantled and harvested for their bricks are located on St. Louis's north side, with a southern boundary of Delmar Road, says RJ Koscielniak, Assistant Professor of Urban and Regional Planning at Eastern Michigan University (who also hails from St. Louis). North of this street, he says, resides the majority of the Black population, while south of Delmar the population is "60-70% white." This was not unintentional: restrictive covenants and a voter-approved segregation ordinance ensured such separation.

"Most of the Black population of the St. Louis region lives in North City, but also in the north county suburbs of the city. And there has been white flight that characterized St. Louis, during much of the 20th century," explains Koscielniak. In *Broken Heart*, Johnson points to Harland Bartholomew, the infamous St. Louis city planner who would spend his 37-year career systematically demolishing Black neighborhoods. His 1947 Comprehensive City Plan, "built the infrastructure of white exodus," writes Johnson. Interstate highways he proposed that would connect suburbs with the city, and numerous downtown parking garages that would accommodate the, "quarter million vehicles he imagined would be driving more than 2.4 billion miles annually in and out of downtown." The plans, Johnson writes, targeted several, majority-Black hundred-square blocks called Mill Creek Valley, just north of Delmar, for destruction and were soon demolished. The decline ensued: Between 1950 and 2000, St. Louis lost more than half its population to surrounding suburban areas; since 2000 that decline has approached 70%.

From Mill Creek Valley to the nearby Pruitt-Igoe public housing development that was built in 1954 and demolished twenty years later, North City's built environment has been characterized by a history of racialization that has led to abandonment. One can examine the effects of racialized abandonment in the North City neighborhood—buildings in mid-collapse, hollowed-out shells colored by overgrown shrubs. Some of those houses still standing are missing exterior walls; on a recent trip, I saw an entire structure sitting open-faced to reveal interior rooms, still partially intact.

These buildings, colloquially called "dollhouses," are evidence of brick theft. The material that built St. Louis, that characterizes the city's vernacular identity, has been quietly disassembled; again, to be sold to build places from scratch. When Koscielniak was a graduate student at Washington University in St. Louis, he was curious about the brick theft occurring in North City. "When you pass by a vacant residential structure in St. Louis and it's missing a wall or it looks like the roof is caved in, it's because somebody stole that building. The idea that somebody is stealing buildings is pretty provocative. And so I started looking deeper into it," he says.

He found that abandoned buildings were becoming targets of savvy groups who would use a variety of tactics to disassemble a building. To steal a building, one could simply back a truck or large van into a building to loosen walls and facades; or, a more damaging trick, to start fires in abandoned buildings.

"Because of how tight and dense a lot of the historic built environment in St. Louis is, when the fire department shows up, they hose down all of the adjacent buildings because they don't want the fire to jump from structure to structure. And while this has the effect of ideally preventing that fire from spreading, it also loosens all of the mortar on these structures," he explains. "After the authorities have left, brick harvesters will show up and they will take their haul and then they will end up at a brick yard." Koscielniak was able to track the supply chain from St. Louis to Sunbelt cities like Phoenix and Atlanta.

Sumell also heard about those stolen bricks ending up in a project much closer to her New Orleans home: from that *99% Invisible* episode, she learned about the repurposing of stolen brick in houses designed by the architect A. Hays Town—located in Baton Rouge.

"St. Louis had a brick industry that distributed bricks across the Midwest, which is also different from the brick industry that destroyed and extracted value from Black homes and sold those downstream to build neo-plantation-style homes," Sumell says. Much of this stolen brick, says Allen, is used to build decorative pavers, retaining walls, or non-load bearing facades. But Koscielniak believes that while it's easy to be sympathetic toward the need to preserve the city's iconic brick and criminalize those "harvesters,", that sympathy obscures a far more complicated issue.

"Most of the narrative around this was anti-poor rhetoric. To reduce the problem of St. Louis's salvaged or stolen brick issue to these bad actors who are just trying to exploit the built environment, it ignores the fact that the vast majority of demolitions in St. Louis are permanent and official, and those bricks still end up in Phoenix," he says.

While so much ire has been concentrated on the 'unofficial' disassembly (brick 'theft'), he says, Koscielniak's research this summer confirms that contractors, "don't charge for taking down specific buildings" or intentionally reduce their demolition rates knowing that they will sell the bricks after demolition. "There are all these records of demolition contracts being approved at zero dollars, because these contractors are essentially saying, 'This is a six family structure, we're going to sell the bricks, put the bricks into the supply chain, we will make fifty grand,'" he says. It's a lucrative business: Koscielniak notes that while Detroit, in the past ten year period, has "roughly 16" demolition contractors working with the city, St. Louis has had 168. "It's much easier just to sell the bricks as the profit or income stream, than it is to actually deal with with a bidding process. Which basically means that everybody's accepted that the land has zero value." The land, he continues, has virtually no value until the building that sits on that land is dismantled.

"Having a market for these reclaimed materials, you're actually incentivizing the unsustainability of many of the neighborhoods in St. Louis, actively encouraging converting 'low value property' or 'no-value property' into valuable property through the dismantling process, and then shipping that across the country where it can be enrolled in speculative development projects without taking into account how this process of development is really dependent on a continued process of disruption, formal or informal, in St. Louis," he adds.

The problem is not the theft itself; it is about how the city of St. Louis has systematically devalued the people who inhabited the land for generations and used their dispossession as a means to create value for wealthy individuals—not dissimilar from the settler colonial conquest of the Missouri valley.

So when tasked with interpreting this dispossession-to-development pipeline that began with the displacement of native people and ends with 21st-century construction, Sumell titled her project *Freesoilparty*—a nod to the short-lived, Manifest Destiny-era abolitionists of the Free Soil Party.

"They were a political party that moved from upstate New York to St. Louis because St. Louis at this moment was this gateway to the west, and their one single platform political issue was was that they wanted the West to be a slavery free zone," says Puleo. Their motto, "Free soil, free men, free land" struck Sumell with the irony of removing indigenous peoples from their physical land under the guise of freedom; "free soil" becomes the material—red clay—only made 'free' by violent conquest. But the violent dispossession of indigenous peoples was inherently connected to these ideologies of abolition.

"In this abolitionist platform they're perpetuating: on one hand, trying to ameliorate the white supremacy of slavery but by perpetuating the white supremacy of settler colonialism and asking freedmen to participate in the dispossession of native people," says Puleo. "So it's bringing along of formerly enslaved or an abolition of slavery that is still built into settler colonialism."

With *Freesoilparty*, Sumell will return bricks harvested from St. Louis back to the earth. Working with brickyards, she acquired dozens of St. Louis Red Queens—a larger version of the common red brick dating back to the 19th century. Each brick was destroyed, crushed by hand or by a steamroller, rendered into dust. Then, the brick was mixed with soils and native seeds, and dispersed throughout the Midwest. The is what curator Puleo calls, "rematriation."

Repatriation, says Puleo, wouldn't address the historic injustices in St. Louis—repatriation means returning objects to their cultural patrimony. For them to repatriate the bricks to St. Louis would mean to rebuild the homes that were destroyed. "This idea that we would re-materialize something that would stay materialized didn't seem to be like the right sort of material consequence," she explains. "But at the same time it was also not the same ethical consequence." By rematriating the bricks—by returning them to the earth—Sumell could grapple with the more insidious layers of theft that occurred in and around the bricks, including the land theft during settler conquest, and the theft of wealth from Black residents.

The process was laborious and physically challenging, but resulted in performances held at the site of the former Du-Good Chemicals—a St. Louis-based, Black-owned chemical manufacturer who, says Sumell, produced both ingredients for pest control but also anti-cancer therapeutics. The owner, Lincoln Duiguid, was a key figure in the community, providing living-wage jobs and youth mentorship. After the bricks were crushed and mixed, Sumell will distribute the concoctions back to the former clay mines, and work with St. Louis artist William Travis, who works in rehabilitating pollinator spaces.

Through rematriation, Sumell hopes she can attend to past injustices through liberation—of soil itself, and prescribed economic value systems. While there is no 'undoing,' of injustice, Puleo says, there is, however, a space to 'do differently.' "I think that's what Jackie is trying to do differently with these bricks, by taking them out of commerce, taking them out of a site where they continue to extract or accumulate value… put [bricks] through a different system that they can literally change the idea of value around the bricks to something that can be generative." Like her anti-carceral practice, we are invited to imagine freedom, liberation, and justice through the earth and its flora.

Walking down Cass Avenue in St. Louis's North City, I came across a building without a front facade. It was laid out upon the ground: rust-colored brick spilled from a large pile and thinned out toward the street. I picked up one brick, broken in half. It was hefty for its size—about six-inches across, just small enough to palm—and it glimmered from the earlier day's rain. I put that half-brick in my pocket, and kept on walking.

The Great Cougar Comeback

PATRICK SHEA

The following story is adapted from an episode of Points North, a narrative podcast about the land, water, and inhabitants of the Great Lakes. Listen to more episodes at pointsnorthpodcast.org.

The small town of Hillsboro sits at the bottom of a valley, surrounded by steep wooded hills. It's probably not what comes to mind when you think of southern Wisconsin. These woods are scattered with boulders, cliffs and caves.

Growing up in Hillsboro, this terrain was Steve Stanek's playground.

"Back when I was a kid, there was no such thing as no trespassing. You could go anywhere you wanted to—out in the country, or the woods and the hills," Stanek said. "There's a large bluff that towers above Hillsboro. It didn't really have a name, but we called it Spook Bluff."

One day, when Steve was 13, he and some friends were exploring the woods on top of Spook Bluff.

"We came down off one side of it and stopped at a farm to get a drink of water, and this enormous roar came out of the woods," Stanek said. "It was loud, it was throaty, you know; deep."

Unsure what he had just heard, Stanek hurried home, a little shook up.

Twenty years later, he was working as a reporter at a local newspaper.

"One of our type-setters…had seen a large tan cougar on her property," Stanek said. "That was the first one. And when you hear of one, you become aware of another and another and another."

Once he asked around, the local sightings started flooding in—and haven't stopped since. He's been on the cougar beat for over 30 years now.

"I've published over the years probably about 200 sightings," said Stanek. "I would say over 50% of them were black."

The thing is, a black cougar has never been documented by wildlife biologists anywhere.

"There's no such thing as a black cougar," said Stanek. "They don't exist. But are they here? Yes."

There are things we see and hear, and then there are the things that science can confirm. This is a story about the tug-of-war between them, and how that tension might make it harder to find the truth.

WISCONSIN'S BLACK CAT CAPITAL

"Hidden gem" is a term so overused that it's sort of lost its meaning. But I can't think of a better way to describe the Driftless Area.

During the last ice age, a chunk of land about the size of West Virginia was missed by the glaciers that leveled the rest of the Midwest. So instead of the flat farmland you'd expect, there are rocky bluffs and huge hills. As a flatlander, I'd call them borderline mountains.

That's why Steve Stanek thinks it's a perfect place for wildcats.

"There's plenty of places for these things to build dens and to hide," Stanek said. "To me there's no mystery about this at all," said Stanek. "I think they're year-round residents here, and have always been. I think there's tons of evidence here."

Steve wanted to show me that evidence. First stop: Sue Wallace, who says she saw a black cougar right in her driveway a couple years ago. So, we went for a drive.

Perfect habitat for a mountain lion? Wooded bluffs like this one south of Hillsboro, WI, can be found throughout the Driftless Area. (Patrick Shea / Points North)

It was strangely warm—a rainy day in the middle of January. The melting snow turned to fog that seemed to get tangled in the treetops. It was the kind of day when you'd expect to see something mysterious.

Steve told me Sue was a little nervous about being recorded. That's natural. But she agreed, probably because Steve is here. Everywhere we went, he got a warm reception. People are glad he's reporting on these sightings, because they're looking for an explanation.

A lot of folks say they've seen these big black cats. And as we drove down a backroad winding through the hills, I peered into the fog and I saw one, too.

We pulled over for a closer look at a wooden cutout of a huge black cat, displayed along the side of an old, white barn—a la bigfoot.

"It shows you how there's the notoriety of this area, especially this valley," Stanek said. "There's been so many sightings here."

We turned onto Sue Wallace's dirt driveway, which runs up the middle of a ravine with wooded slopes rising up from both sides of the two-track.

Wallace has lived in Hillsboro her whole life. She's lived at this beautiful spot west of town for eight years, along with her husband, kids, cats, dogs, and some donkeys. Sue said a few months ago, her husband noticed the donkeys getting really riled up about something in the woods. She has a guess at what it was.

Because one November morning, before sunrise, Wallace saw something she'll never forget.

"The truck was parked up there in between the two sheds, and then I backed it up down up on the driveway and [came] down here," said Wallace. "And then it just walked right in front of my headlights."

Wallace said a huge black cat slipped silently down the driveway, didn't even glance at her, and disappeared into the darkness.

"His tail just, you know, it swooped like this," said Wallace, making an upward curving motion with her hand. "It was a long tail; kind of a long body, decently sized."

"The dog that we had in the house was 120 pounds, and I thought for a quick second it might have been him," Wallace said. "But then you see the tail on that lion … I ended up sitting in the truck for about 10 minutes before I got out to come in the house. It was pretty scary. Kind of cool though, too."

THE COUGAR BEAT

Stanek said Sue Wallace is just one of hundreds of eyewitnesses near Hillsboro. At a nearby library, we head to the basement where they keep archived newspapers. Steve pulls out a series of articles from his 30 years of reporting on cougar sightings.

"8 PM on the last day of May, 1993, while doing chores on their farm…"

"About 40 yards away I saw this big black cat, he reported. The creature was huge…"

"John compared the size of the lion to a large dog and said it was stone black…"

"I stepped out of the barn and here was this beautiful black, glistening animal, Joanne revealed…

"Johnson dashed into his garage to grab his cell phone for photographic proof 'By the time I got back out, it was gone,' he said. 'I could hear it bounding away through the woods to the southeast.

Steve Stanek says he's reported on over 200 wildcat sightings in local newspapers—with over half the eyewitnesses describing a large, black cat. (Patrick Shea / Points North)

Now remember—scientists have never documented a black mountain lion. So as Stanek published sighting after sighting, he wondered what kind of cats these really were. He thought back to when he was 13, and heard that roar from the woods near Spook Bluff.

"I could describe it exactly, because the next time I heard it was my folks took us to the circus in Madison," Stanek said. "And it was an African Lion. It was the same roar."

Mountain lions—also called pumas, cougars, or catamounts—don't roar. They usually don't make much sound at all, but when they do it's a sort of screech.

In fact, there's only one wildcat native to the western hemisphere that roars at all.

"And that's a jaguar," Stanek said. "And a jaguar would explain a lot."

CRYPTID CATS

Jaguars are in the same family as cougars, but a different genus: Panthera. Experts say they can have a melanistic phase—meaning the jet-black fur that people are describing near Hillsboro.

Stanek believes jaguars and cougars started mating, and have hybridized in the Driftless Area. And even though the closest known jaguar population is in Mexico, he doesn't need something to officially exist to know it's there.

"I don't know if you're familiar with the term cryptozoology," Stanek said. "I'm familiar with a lot of that stuff. It's the study of possibly unknown or out-of-place animals."

Or as one dictionary puts it—"cryptozoology: the study of creatures, such as the Loch Ness monster, whose existence has not been scientifically proven."

"I don't know for sure if there's such a thing as sasquatch or not," said Stanek. "But the one I give the most credence to are sea serpents."

Steve said he also had a big flying saucer phase in his younger years, and that his whole jaguar beat comes from that life-long fascination with the unknown or unacknowledged.

But in the Midwest, wildcats bridge the gap between "crypto" and actual zoology.

COUGARS ON THE MOVE

There was a time when "mountain lion" wasn't really a fitting name for North America's most iconic wildcat. Cougars once lived all over the continent; not just in the mountains out west.

But like so many other large predators, they were hunted aggressively starting in the 1800s and eradicated from most of the country. There hasn't been a breeding population in the Great Lakes region since the early 1900s, according to wildlife officials.

This mountain lion, photographed in late December, was Wisconsin's 15th confirmed sighting in 2022. (Wisconsin DNR)

But cougars are making a comeback. Slowly but surely, they're coming down from the mountains and moving east again. There's a breeding population back in the Dakotas and Nebraska after being gone for a century.

And even the Wisconsin Department of Natural Resources has confirmed fifteen cougar sightings over the past year. Six of those were in the Driftless Area—not too far from Hillsboro. All of them tan, by the way.

The department says those were all male cougars that walked more than 800 miles from South Dakota.

These animals are very territorial—especially males—and they will travel huge distances in search of a mate. The DNR says they won't find one here, but how are the cougars supposed to know that?

You probably wouldn't know if you're seeing a male or female cougar at first glance. Researchers find that out later, with DNA samples from scat or deer carcasses. But you'd think you'd be able to tell what color it is.

It was still dark that morning when the alleged cougar crossed Sue Wallace's driveway, but she's sure of what she saw.

"It was the black one," Wallace said. "I mean, he walked right in front of my headlights of the truck. I could definitely see what it was."

Despite all the eyewitness accounts, the Wisconsin DNR stands firm in its position: there's no evidence of black cougars in the state. But Stanek thinks state officials know more than they're letting on about.

"The only thing that makes a mystery out of these animals being here is the DNR," Stanek said. "I believe they've live-collared the black ones, along with the tan ones, and released them with radio transmitters."

I pressed Stanek on what the motivation would be for this secretive monitoring. He had a theory for that.

"It's because they don't want to reserve timberland," Stanek said. "Because if this is confirmed that it was an endangered resource, they would have to set land aside."

"I don't know where exactly that stems from," said Randy Johnson, a large carnivore specialist with the Wisconsin DNR. "I think it's probably a bigger issue of mistrust of government and conspiracy, that type of thing. But what I can say is obviously there's no cover up underway. We work really hard, in fact, to share this information."

The DNR has a website dedicated to cougar sightings. There are photos, a map of where the sightings were, a timeline of the DNR's response, and a place to file your own report.

"So, there's really no cover up when we have a web page dedicated to sharing information on them," Johnson said.

When it comes to the black cougars, Johnson was actually careful not to rule it out entirely.

"I think scientifically speaking, there's no reason to think it's not possible," Johnson said, adding that the lack of any official documentation makes him dubious.

"It's never been documented in hunting records; it's never been documented through photographs. There's no evidence of ever having a black phase mountain lion," Johnson said. "However, I think it is possible because there's several species of cats that have a black phase. Never say never, right?"

THE EYES DECEIVE

While Hillsboro seems to be a hotspot for alleged black cougar sightings, they're not limited to just Wisconsin.

In August 2022, someone got a photograph of the black feline creature in Copemish, Michigan. It went viral from there.

DNR officials went to the location with the photographer who took the shots of the black cat. They reenacted the pictures for perspective, placing an item where the cat was spotted. With the data they collected, officials came to the conclusion it was just a housecat, 20-30 inches long.

Despite all the hype, there's still no hard evidence of a black cougar anywhere. And in Michigan, just like Wisconsin, there's been no evidence of a breeding population of even the verified tan cougars since the early 1900s.

But that doesn't mean people stopped seeing them here, either.

"My mom says she saw one, my uncle claims he saw one. But, you know, we just never had any solid evidence," said Brian Roell.

Roell is a lifelong Michigander who's now a wildlife biologist, and part of the DNR's cougar team.

"Any sighting that comes in, that whole team reviews it," Roell said. "And in order for us to call it a confirmed sighting, we have to have a unanimous decision."

A mountain lion captured on a trail camera near Cassville, WI.
(Wisconsin DNR)

"So, we'll actually google cougar pictures, you know, 'cougar next to road' and just do a global search," Roell said. "And then all of a sudden you're like, 'hey, that's the same picture.'"

Since the cougar team's first year in 2008, the number of confirmed sightings has been trending up. And that doesn't necessarily mean there are more cougars; just more sightings.

"I know one thing that has really probably increased our sighting rate is the availability and the use of trail cameras," Roell said. "They are just everywhere out in the woods. Geez, now they've got 'em where they send pictures to your cell phone."

When the cougar team gets a picture that seems promising, they follow up in the field. Most of the team members have traveled to New Mexico and other western states to get trained in tracking these cats. They studied paw prints, scat, and the physical characteristics that separate cougars from animals often mistaken for them.

"I mean, there are a lot of domestic cats that get submitted as mountain lions, Roell said. "We've had a calico even one time. I was like, 'All right now…you know, they do not come in calico.' And by and large, most of those are people that honestly, truly believe they saw a cougar."

There are two different kinds of knowing when it comes to these wildcat sightings. There are eyewitness accounts, of which there's no shortage, and then there's the much smaller pool of sightings confirmed by scientists—with DNA proof, or an unmistakable set of tracks. Different people value these kinds of knowing differently.

But Roell says it's important for the experts to hear folks out. The cougar team tries to be as transparent as possible in their interactions with eyewitnesses. But there's another kind of report that's muddying the water.

"It's one of the weird things that with all our other wildlife sightings, we don't get people doing hoaxes. But with mountain lions, we do," Roell said. "Submitting pictures from other states, we've had mounted cats placed out in the woods before; I know Wisconsin has had the same scenario, so, it's kind of strange."

One incident that stands out to Roell is when a woman in the Upper Peninsula sent in a picture of a cougar, which she says she took from her car.

"She had a young daughter in her car with her, and her young daughter collaborated the story as well," Roell said.

"Yet, what we found out was that the picture was actually shot in Louisiana and was flipped just using Photoshop or whatever. They just inverted the picture and turned the cougar the other way. It just shocked me that she, one, went to that effort but then actually involved her young child in the hoax."

Roell said that's just one of many attempted hoaxes. He's seen cases where people made their own tracks with their thumb. And after the Louisiana photo hoax, he always makes sure to do a thorough internet search before going any further with a reported sighting.

"So, we'll actually Google cougar pictures, you know, 'Cougar next to road' and just do a global search," Roell said. "And then all of a sudden, you're like, 'Hey, that's the same picture.'"

THE COST OF FALSE SIGHTINGS

Roell said he's not sure why someone would do this and neither am I. Sometimes people can be mysterious, too.

But as far as the misidentified sightings, I can see how that might happen. Except maybe the calico.

Over the past few weeks, working on this story, I've become pretty obsessed with mountain lions. If something large and feline darted across the road in front of my headlights, I could see myself coming to the cougar conclusion. Seriously. And so many people do. Roell said his team reviews around 250 sightings per year, but have only ever confirmed 89 ever.

Hillsboro, WI is a hotspot for reported black cougar sightings—an animal never documented by wildlife officials. (Patrick Shea / Points North)

I came into this with a lighthearted story in mind and it is, for the most part. But this deluge of false reports that biologists have to sift through—that takes time. And time is a limited resource. In fact, some of Roell's bosses don't think it's worth it.

"We're getting pressure not to confirm mountain lions to the extent that we currently do," Roell said. "We're having a meeting with the cougar team and with some folks from Lansing to say, 'Is this worth our effort to continue to go through this level of detail?' In my mind, the answer is yes, but I may get overruled on that."

The less trust there is between the experts studying these cats and the folks reporting sightings, the harder it is to keep track of the cougar's expanding range. Roell said it's best when eyewitnesses and scientists work together.

Because a time could come in the not-so-distant future when they could be tracking the true return of cougars to the Midwest.

"We certainly have the habitat to sustain a few mountain lions; I don't think we're ever going to have a really robust population just because they have super large territories," Roell said. "But I think it certainly is in the realm of possibilities."

With a creature as elusive as a mountain lion, it's never easy to definitively say where they are, or where they're going. For now, they live somewhere in this foggy land between myth and migration.

MEMORY & REFLECTION

Forgetting How to Swim

DEMETRIUS BUCKLEY

In the small prison yard, I give Gil a powerful embrace.

"Damn, bro, I ain't get no hug?" Raphael says. "All this favoritism…"

"Here he go, acting like a baby," I joke.

We are back together at Baraga, friends reuniting, discussing what made history in a system that raised men. Lake Superior is down the street, its maritime scent mocking the yard.

"Meech, you crazy as hell," Raphael says, laughing. "How you hear dude say he 'bout to do something to you when you was in your cell, and dude downstairs in his cell?"

"You irritating already. I told you what I heard."

"You need to get your ears checked," Raphael jokes.

"Meech got PTSD," Gil responds. "Prison tore us all up into confetti. But what you finna do when you get home?"

"I've been working on rapping, writing songs," Raphael says, "but if not, I'll get a job, be legit."

"You're going to have to fix yourself, lil bro. The world will wear on you—the women, the freedom, the drugs."

Out the group Gil had a life without parole, but acted as if going home nestled in every tomorrow. My twenty-year sentence was down to eight. Raphael had two months before release, before feeling the solid ground away from this seashore of prison.

"You're done drowning. Don't test the waters no more," Gil says.

"Imma show y'all I can do it. Watch."

Arrested at eighteen, Raphael did thirteen years inside a system full of angry, manipulative men and made it through unscathed. I'd taken a liking to Raphael seven years ago, a slow buildup from when we first met at Baraga, where he was too playful, goofy. I was guarded from any camaraderie, serious about taking control of my life, realizing my wrong decision-making. I'd left my family for friends, for an honor that got lost as soon as I was caught.

Raphael had made himself the little brother in the group. He wasn't aiming to impress like other guys his age, thinking violence was a quick remedy to everything. Raphael was spirited, and I scolded him for keeping a smile on his face, trying to put one on mine. We'd argue over who had better songs on our MP3 players. I was the old-school R&B king, and he'd sneak songs off my player, bounce at his cell door to the smooth jazz in his headphones, a song that came out when he was two years old, swearing he knew about the artist.

"I know about The Whispers— 'This is what I do to get you in the mood,'" he'd sing out the crack of his door.

"Niggah, you got that from me!" I'd say.

"Okay. Okay. What about"—he picked another song from his catalogue, my catalogue—"Al Hudson and Oneway, that uhh, uhh—"

"Cutie Pie!" I'd reclaim.

Gil would come to his door, flatfoot, no socks, because the state didn't issue socks for his big feet. "Meech stole that from me, and Raphael, you stole that from Meech—both y'all some copycats."

We would laugh so hard in a place not meant for laughter, feel family in a place not meant for home. We had built a brotherhood in a place meant only to be punitive.

Thirty-three days before Raphael's release, the prison counselor calls his name over the P.A. He misses yard, oddly quiet the rest of day. We learn in sign language through the glass slit that his grandfather died. Now, that happy home will be met with grief, a cringing heartache— enough to derail a fresh mind back to crime. A loved one dying while we are imprisoned, months away from home, is like seeing the family member on shore and having to swim to them with our unit on our backs. I see his grandfather waving in the night. The unit bobs in some dark ocean, Raphael kicking his legs, coming up for air. Almost home.

Day thirty on the yard, Raphael turns away from the other prisoners, faces the fence to where the water curls against the land. He cries. Gil and I stand in front of him; it's the lake four blocks away, the unfreezing surface releasing what we left behind. It's the building he holds, the system digging into his aching shoulders. I too turn toward the fence, add to the ocean, to the sorrow.

Day twenty, they are packing Raphael up to be transferred closer to Detroit. He's making it to shore. Raphael yells up the hall, "Gil. Meech,

I love y'all. Imma keep in touch!"

"Stay focused," I yell.

And just like that he's gone. Life feels duller, harder. After Gil transfers to a different facility, I stay to myself, wondering if Raphael made it out in the world with his courage, his joyfulness. I don't care if he keeps in contact; I prefer him not to relive this place. Most don't reach back and that doesn't mean the bond isn't genuine. It isn't any different than a relative; they always forget to reach out.

At the emailing kiosk, a couple months after Raphael left, I click on the flashing icon: (20) messages. *Here's my number*, one says. *Call me.* I open the picture and it's Raphael, dreads hanging over his face, looking clean. Energy bolts through me, then a fear I can't quite explain. I become impatient to call him, thinking he's fallen into a life of crime, testing those waters. The shoes, clothes, and money fanned in a half circle set it off. When I finally make it outside to call, I dial the wrong number. Start over. The small paper inked with numbers blows in the breeze. The second dial my fingers hit the right numbers. A long wait.

"What's up, bro!"

"Remember this place—don't come back—don't..." My voice vibrates from my kicking legs, from readjusting the building on my shoulder.

"I'm not doing anything illegal. I gotta record deal!"

"Get da fuck outta here!"

"For real. I gotta take care of Grams, honor my grandpop, and look out for y'all... family."

The building on my back chips off a section in the water, a splash beside me. I see Raphael at shore, waving, waiting.

My mouth stretches across my face. "That's good to hear." My worries seem smaller than before. After our talk, my mind spins on how big he'd get, putting Detroit on the map; Raphael has a promising future now. Splash.

Two months elapse without hearing from him, a busy man with a record deal, but like clockwork on the yard I show the pictures Raphael sent me to a few guys. I show off his success, what any friend does to feel connected, important.

"Lil bro out there getting it."

The sun is shining on this ocean, the brick buildings drying as we hold them above our heads.

"I know Raphael," someone says. "He got that song with Icewear Vezzo."

"Yeah, that's my little bro. I'm 'bout to call him in a minute."

"You know he dead, right? For a month now."

I gaze up. "He ain't dead. Look." I surf through the pictures where he's alive. We dispute over Raphael's life, his wellbeing, same as I did when he was inside. He is so far on shore, making something of himself, and them, us, in prison with buildings on our backs, swimming, drowning, screaming out a mouthful of water. My lil bro ain't dead.

I call several times the next day, but I get no answer. I try his grandmother. Water in my mouth, legs kicking.

"Hello, this is Demetrius, a friend of Raphael." I hear seagulls circle. "Is he okay?"

Her voice rasps. "Baby, Raphael dead. He took a pill with fentanyl in it, maybe didn't know it was in there. Went to sleep, never woke up."

I listen with everything in me, hope to hear him in the background, some grand joke of his.

"They wanted him dead, was jealous. We weren't all slaves and pitiful black folks they show on TV. Don't take that vision into your mind, that's how they get you." She goes on as if I am Raphael, back somewhere she knew he'd be. "When you wake up, if you wake up...you better be careful."

"Yes, ma'am." She's my grandmother now, teaching me what not to do. I am Raphael.

"We're putting his music on YouTube. ATM Simba his rap name. You check back with me, OK?"

After a few more words we hang up. What his grandmother said about the jealousy of people who'd pull him back in that life is true. I never anticipated him dying while making something of himself. I had been too worried he would come back to prison, but entering into a new world is like learning to walk again with sea legs. I'll drown tonight, wake tomorrow, and see Raphael's grandmother waving me to keep swimming...if I wake.

Kindness is its Own Memory

LORI JAKIELA

This story involves bad pantyhose and poor sports reportage, but it also involves Franco Harris and another link on his chain of good deeds. Back in the late 1980s, I worked for Penn State—Franco Harris's alma mater. I worked in public relations and sports information, despite knowing almost nothing about sports. My bosses were 1980s power-suit women who saw themselves as mentors for clueless marshmallow neophytes like me.

My bosses taught me a lot of hard lessons - how important it was for women to wear make-up, but not too much make-up; how essential it was for women to smile, but not smile too much. They taught me the power of shoulder pads that could double as oven mitts, the importance of learning to walk in heels that could stand in as weapons in James Bond films, and how kindness is often misunderstood as weakness.

"Ice that crap over," my one boss said about on-the-job feelings.

"Hold the tears for people who care enough to pass the Kleenex," my other boss said, a mantra I think she practiced in mirrors and wrote on Post-It notes she stuck to her fridge.

The 1980s were strange times. When I was hired at Penn State to do Penn State things, pantyhose were required for women. L'eggs pantyhose were favorites, in colors called Suntan and Nude. They came in plastic eggs, like every new pair was hatching something wonderful.

I forget what my bosses said about pantyhose, but it was understood that naked legs were as off-limits as feelings on the job.

One day, at a golf-outing fundraiser, I had a raging fever. I hardly ever ran a fever, so I was sure I was dying. I was sweaty and woozy and incapable of raising any funds unless the funds I was raising were for my own coffin.

This was summer, so the pantyhose I was obliged to wear stuck to my legs like a layer of wax. I plucked at them, trying to get a little air in. My bosses saw me plucking and sweating and were livid. I was an embarrassment and, possibly, a fiscal disaster.

Enter Franco Harris.

Franco - Penn State's star running back and sweetheart. Pittsburgh Steelers' star running back and sweetheart. He must have seen I was close to passing out. He must have seen through the smile I'd pasted on because this was my first real job, and because I wanted to be the kind of woman who was tough enough to smile but not too much, to wear make-up, but not too much, and because I very much did not want to be fired.

Franco stepped between me and one of my bosses.

He said, "Sweetheart, you don't look so good."

I can't remember what I said to him. Everything is a bit fuzzy, fever and all, but kindness is its own memory, folding over an otherwise lost moment like a blanket.

Still, I remember Franco, that lovely huge man, my hometown legend. He took me by the arm, right in front of my boss, who glared but couldn't argue.

Franco took me to a car. I think it was a nice car. Black, shiny. He put me in the backseat, where there was a cooler filled with popsicles.

Franco was in the healthy popsicle business back then. He told me to eat a popsicle. Maybe two. He told me his driver would take me home. He said not to worry. He'd smooth things over.

"Just get some rest and get better," he said, and in my fever-frazzled memory, Franco winked.

Dear former bosses:

I think you meant well. Thank you for trying.

Even now, my mascara looks like bed bugs running a relay down my cheeks. Blush makes me look like I've inhaled too much helium. My lips are so thin that TikTok make-up tutorials advise sketching new lips, better lips, with lip pencils, which make me look like the Joker in Batman, but without the murderous gravitas. When I try to walk in heels, I look like Buster Keaton doing a silent-movie stunt. I haven't worn pantyhose for a decade at least, and L'eggs come in boxes now anyway, and what fun is that?

I smile every chance I get. My laugh is loud and sounds a bit crazy, I think. I try to tell the truth because everything else is harder.

Have you read Kurt Vonnegut? I love Kurt Vonnegut, who said there's only one rule in this life: "Be kind, babies."

Kurt Vonnegut said people should stay soft and not let the world make them hard.

It's good advice. I'm trying to take it.

During the years I held my Penn State job, I failed epically.

I cried once, despite not being a crier, in the office of my Penn State Sports Director, who hated me because he discovered how little I knew about sports. I tried to take stats at a basketball game. It didn't go well.

"Useless," the Sports Director said, and threw some stats sheets and a pen at me and my tears surprised both of us.

Before Penn State, I worked for the *Erie Daily Times* covering sports, but not really. My editors were my college journalism professors, kind men who thought it might be good to have a young woman covering sports.

Maybe I was a diversity hire in the newsroom, though we didn't have that language back then. My editors were simply kind and patient people who believed in me despite evidence to the contrary.

I covered mostly human-interest stories—stories about one-armed bowling champions and blind twins who golfed. I covered stories about Kurt Angle, a local boy and champion wrestler whose story was hard to muck up. When I had to do a real sports story, I'd come to my editors with statistics I didn't understand, and they'd explain the numbers without making me feel like the idiot I was. Then I'd go write, under deadline, pretending to know a thing about a thing I knew nothing about.

I still know little about sports, but I became a writer through the kindness and patience of others.

Like most Pittsburghers, I love the Steelers, despite my limited understanding of football. I grew up watching Franco. I loved that the

Steelers won Super Bowls when Pittsburgh itself was floundering, our mills closing, so many people out of work and hope.

Franco, his toughness and talent, his kindness and patience, his humility and grace gave my city dignity. Franco's goodness became a metaphor for the best of Pittsburgh.

"I'm forever black and gold," Franco liked to say long after his Pittsburgh playing days were over.

———

"It's not a thing of how many carries," Franco said to reporters who asked him again and again about the Immaculate Reception, the one moment that cemented his place in history, the one miracle I watched so many times on TV that I, like millions of other Pittsburgh Steelers fans, felt like I lived it. "But were you effective when you did carry."

———

Dear Franco.

I think he nearly carried me to his car that long-ago day, I was that weak and dizzy.

I got home safe. The popsicle was strawberry, I think, and it was delicious, so cold on my swollen flu-struck tongue. I went to bed and slept the rest of the day.

I didn't get fired. My bosses never said much about it. I think they even treated me a little more gently after that, the way people might treat someone who'd been blessed by the Pope.

When I saw Franco many years later and thanked him, he didn't remember helping me. Why would he? It was a tiny thing. A simple kindness to a clueless kid with the flu. It was, I think, just one in a string of too many kindnesses to count.

Everyone has a Franco story, it seems. Weeks after Franco's passing, I keep reading them—all those times he took a moment to sign an autograph or pose for a picture; all the times he was gentle and patient with fans and other players; the random Franco sightings on the airport shuttle or Pittsburgh sandwich shop.

"It's almost impossible to process that he could give so much to so many people personally," Franco's son, Dok Harris, told ESPN. "People have been telling me stories about how they met him some time in 1977 or 1987 or 1991. It was important to them, and it made a difference in their lives. And that's really the beauty of my father, truly a very blessed soul who just really sought to help everybody out."

I keep thinking of a poem by another of my beloveds, Raymond Carver. The poem is called "Late Fragment."

It goes like this:

And did you get what you wanted from this life even so? I did. And what was it you wanted?

To call myself beloved.

To feel myself beloved on this earth.

Dear Franco:

You are beloved on this earth.

The Accident that Changed a City

ROBERT ISENBERG

Nine years, I think, pedaling a borrowed bicycle down Braddock Avenue, *and so much is the same.*

I coast past familiar storefronts—a cafe, an indie cinema, a mural of birds in flight. Traffic flows around me, leaving a narrow space between moving cars and parked ones. The lawns and trees are exactly as I remember them. My heart throbs, not with exertion, but with love.

"Feel free to take it all day," said my friend Bill, who's hosting me in his spare room and loaned me this bike. He said this during our long night of Yuenglings and pool at the local bar. "I'll text you after work and see where you are."

Even the generosity is the same.

Really, it's only been three years since I last visited Pittsburgh, and I would've been here sooner, if not for COVID-19. But scattered drop-ins are nothing like living here. A decade ago, my wife and I owned a condo in Point Breeze, and that was a good time in our life. I miss so many things, but *this* in particular: cruising around on a wonky bicycle. Soon, I'm flying down my old street, between rows of suburban lots, past the iron gates of my old complex, which looks exactly as I left it.

Today I will ride 27 miles around the city, from the eastern edge of Regent Square to a warehouse district beyond the West End Bridge—basically, across city limits and back. My reunion must be thorough, physical, full-contact. I will explore this city the way I did when I lived here—on two wheels, propelled by my own two legs. My tire will skirt all Three Rivers. I'll cut through about 16 distinct neighborhoods, which I could once fluently navigate. I'll climb nearly 1,000 feet, much of it potholed or paved with cobblestone. The weather is spring-cool. The sky is a merciful blend of clouds and sun. I will treasure every block, because it really has been too long.

But when I arrive in the busy hub of South Oakland, something will happen. Sweat-soaked and achy, I will heave my bike up a long, concrete staircase and emerge from the woods behind the Frick Fine Arts Center. I'll pedal into traffic, making a slow circle around the greensward of Schenley Plaza. And there, beneath the 36-story gothic stonework of the Cathedral of Learning, I'll see it - the Ghost Bike.

The bike, painted white and locked to a steel post, will stand silently on the sidewalk, a memorial to the woman who lost her life here.

And in that moment, I'll take stock of everything that's different. Because it's *not* the same Pittsburgh I remember—and I don't mean new high-rises, shuttered businesses, or graying friends. For a cyclist who's been away for a while, the city exhibits radical transformation. Spotting that Ghost Bike will fill me with anger and heartache. I will wish, for the thousandth time, that this memorial didn't have to exist. But I will also marvel at all the change that began with a single accident. And I will wonder what Susan would think of it all.

I can't exaggerate - Susan Hicks really was one of the kindest and most genuine people I ever met. She really did love to smile, and to laugh, and did both all the time. But the way I remember her is consistently *chill*. Everything she did looked effortless and easygoing, as if she'd just woken up from an afternoon nap. She had straight blond hair and sleepy eyes; her cadence reminded me of snowboarders. Everyone loved her.

Susan and I weren't bosom buddies; there were legions of people who knew her better. But we ran into each other again and again, usually at house parties, for years. My memories are hazy, but some stand out: Talking together about theater for a solid hour on the fire escape of somebody's apartment. Rolling sushi on a butcher block in somebody's kitchen. And yes, once riding bikes around Schenley Park with a posse of friends. Throughout our twenties, Pittsburgh was busy with rooftop shindigs, ersatz music events, and gallery openings. Susan and I were always bumping into each other, and I was always pleased as punch to see her.

Like so many of those friends, Susan was dynamic and whip smart. A Virginia native, Susan had lived in Russia, Serbia, and Puerto Rico. She earned a PhD in anthropology from the University of British Columbia. By her mid-thirties, Susan was assistant director of academic affairs at the Center for Russian and East European Studies, a showcase program at the University of Pittsburgh. She joined a rowing team. She was fluent in the Russian language. She organized regular get-togethers with friends, where they would divvy up roles and read Shakespeare aloud. If anyone deserved to live a long and happy life, it was Susan.

I learned about the accident on my 26th birthday. My Facebook account was littered with posts—alerts, exclamations, updates, and so many woeful comments, a new one every few minutes. If social media could wail in anguish, it wailed that day.

The facts emerged: Susan was riding her bike down Forbes Avenue, a major artery in Pittsburgh. She routinely commuted to work, and Forbes was one of her regular routes. Out of nowhere, a car collided with her bike; she was "pinned," according to reports, an image I refuse to let myself imagine. Susan was critically injured. She was rushed to a hospital, but it was too late to save her.

The driver, it turned out, was high on synthetic marijuana. He didn't have a license. When police arrived, he allegedly "faked a seizure." In press photos, the man is unkempt, his expression inscrutably grim. His face contrasted sharply with Susan's beaming portrait. But there they were, paired together on the evening news, killer and victim, forever bound in each other's tragic story. That face would reappear six months later, when the driver was arrested, and again in 2017, when he was sentenced to five-and-a-half to nine years in prison for involuntary manslaughter.

"Death of cyclist, Pitt educator leaves hole in community," read a headline in the Pittsburgh Tribune Review.

A hole, yes. There was no better word for it.

The accident proved something that everyone knew, but no City Council had ever really addressed: Pittsburgh was a deadly place for cyclists.

When I returned from my freshman year of college, in the summer of 1998, I asked my Dad to look at the bicycle I'd ridden around Pitt's campus. The hybrid was only a year old, but now that it stood upside down in my parents' garage in rural Vermont, it looked scratched and weatherbeaten.

"I can't believe it," said my Dad, "but I think we have to replace these brake pads."

I nodded, not understanding.

"*I don't think I've replaced my brake pads once in ten years,*" Dad elaborated. He spun the front rim and squeezed a brake lever, but all I heard was a wheezing sound; the wheel continued to whirl. "You must use these *a lot.*"

And so, it dawned on me - Pittsburgh is a city of *very* hard stops.

I lived in Pittsburgh for fifteen more years, and for most of them, I didn't drive at all. I rode the bus and bummed *a lot* of rides; but I also pumped my trusty hybrid all over town. And at every blind corner; rolling down every treacherous slope; through every blinking yellow light, I took my life into my own hands.

Because Pittsburgh was one of the worst-rated cities for cyclists, and many of its challenges persist. The streets are a maze. The hills are punishing. The pavement itself is cracked and pockmarked. Intersections are Kafka-esque. Even major roads are narrow and crowded with parked cars. Meanwhile, storms can pour for days, and freezing rain falls all winter. Gutters clog with jetsam; frost heaves rip open the pavement. Even the sidewalks are comically uneven.

In my memory, only true zealots commuted by bike, and they always seemed to dress the part: tattooed hipsters, flying around corners on customized fixies, flipping off drivers as horns honked all around them. We were odd ducks, pedaling over bridges and cutting through alleyways, narrowly missing side mirrors in our quest to get somewhere on time. I was no tattooed hipster, but the chaotic vibe matched the defiant headspace of my youth. I *liked* the danger. Riding untamed streets thrilled me to the marrow. Sure, I would've loved bike lanes and special signals, dedicated bridges and convenient racks; but these things were never going to exist, so I might as well accept the blow-by-blow threats of coma and paralysis. *Go ahead, Steel City. Bring it.*

Susan's accident changed all that, for me and for everyone. Fighting traffic wasn't a game, or a badge of courage, or even a statement. People could die. Someone *had* died. And not just someone, but an exceptional someone, a person so cool and beloved that her passing couldn't be ignored. The streets themselves were unsafe at any speed.

And for the first time, the landscape truly began to change.

———————————

Morning becomes noon. I ride a rail-trail along the Allegheny River, passing woods and gray water. In the North Side, I find a network of bike lanes painted on the street. I pass a special parking platform for bikes, where attractive new racks stand in ranks. Some of these I remember, but so much is new. In the crisp air, I can almost smell the paint.

Noon becomes afternoon. I ascend a concrete ramp onto the Fort Pitt Bridge and coast into Point State Park. *Cyclists are everywhere*, zipping up and down the braid of paths. Then I glide into Downtown, where I find bike lane after bike lane, the white lines crisply printed on the asphalt.

Like most urban networks, this route isn't a straight line; it's more like a high-speed scavenger hunt. I lose my way several times, making awkward U-turns over sidewalks and parking lots. I slip between skyscrapers, zigzagging my way toward the next rail-trail. I spot a pair of signs bolted to a post: "Do Not Enter," followed by "Except [Picture of a Bicycle]." And I laugh aloud.

Don't get me wrong - activists have been fighting for bicycle safety in Pittsburgh for decades. In 2002, a rider named David Hoffman was deliberately sideswiped by a passing car. His story earned widespread media attention and support from fellow cyclists. Within a year, Hoffman had cofounded BikePGH, a cycling advocacy group, with Scott Bricker and Lou Fineberg. For the past 20 years, BikePGH has been a vocal champion of urban mobility. BikePGH created Free Ride, a bike-recycling program; printed the Pittsburgh Bike Map; and commissioned the installation of bike racks all over town, including on every Port Authority bus. Like so many American cities, Pittsburgh was already taking steps in the right direction, thanks to a feisty activist community.

But it's fair to say that Susan's accident radically accelerated the process. The Pennsylvania House Transportation Committee unanimously passed House Bill 140 in 2021, but anyone familiar with the bill knows it as "Susan and Emily's Law." The bill is also named after Emily Fredericks, a Philadelphia resident killed in a similar collision. In short, the law makes it easier to install bike lanes on urban streets. The implication, of course, is that Susan and Emily would still be alive if they could have ridden on this kind of protected pavement. What a difference a few feet might have made.

Not everyone likes the new infrastructure. Parking has always been awful, they carp, and the bike lanes make it worse. The streets are a convoluted mess of one-way streets and last-second lane changes, and all that white-and-green paint makes it even more confusing. Among politicians, bike safety is a favorite political shuttlecock. When a friend of mine recently posted a picture of himself riding his bike down the street, someone commented: "BIKE LANES ARE THE DEVIL."

I get it—they see another roadblock in a city full of roadblocks. I see a city that is finally taking its quality of life seriously, at least in a way that I value. But one thing can't be argued - Susan should be alive, and isn't.

In Oakland, not far from Susan's ghost bike, I find that long, concrete staircase behind the Frick Fine Arts Center. I heave the bike onto my shoulder, so I can carry it up the fifty-or-so steps. I did this hundreds of times, back when I lived in Pittsburgh; bikeable roadways would end, and I'd have to lug my frame up and down this kind of stairway. It ain't easy, but it's comforting. The 800-or-so outdoor stairways are iconic landmarks, a century-old accommodation for workers commuting on foot.

But then I notice something: a little picture of a bicycle, embedded in the cement.

This staircase has a ramp. I fit my tires on the little shelf; soon, the bike is rolling upward. To push a bicycle is so much easier than lifting it, and I marvel at this clever little channel. I stomp my way up, breathing hard. These are the little additions that make a big difference.

Understand, I would trade all these things to bring Susan back to life. Without question. The lanes, the paths, the racks cleverly shaped like the Golden Triangle—none of it will ever be worth losing her.

But I think Susan would have liked what Pittsburghers have done. The strides they've taken. She would be amazed what this city has achieved since her passing. Lives have been saved, more lives than we'll ever know.

I reach the top of the hill, set the bike down, and ride. And keep riding, as long as I can.

Exiles Living in a Church

KRISTIN KOVACIC

. . . Blessed are they that dwell in thy house, O Lord: they shall praise thee for ever and ever.—Psalm 83

St. Matthew, Apostle and Evangelist

Thanksgiving 2021, and our daughter Rosalie has come home to Pittsburgh from D.C. Only the celebration, as it was last year, has been ruined by the pandemic. Our son and his partner are marooned in Brazil. My sister's family is exposed—Delta the strain of the moment—and her hosting of the traditional family gathering scratched at the last minute.

Only we aren't truly "home," either. My husband and I have recently retired from teaching, downsized, and moved across town, shedding most of the worldly goods we accumulated over thirty-five years in a sagging, six-bedroom house in Pittsburgh's East End to squeeze into a two-bedroom condo in a new development of a 100-year-old church on the South Side.

It was a challenging transition, still in progress. Among the challenges for me is the suspicion that I've gotten off easy and am not suffering to the degree that everyone else in the ravaged world around me seems to be. The price of the condo alone makes me feel ill, not just with buyers' remorse, but with a nauseating awareness of the precise amount of our fortune, however hard-earned.

Furniture suitable for this compact "loft" has not yet arrived (supply chain issues being another feature of the plague), and so our little trinity hovers around the glossy quartz kitchen island, fashioned in the shape and rough location of the church's original altar, and expresses gratitude over leftover Thai takeout and my sad side dish of squash.

We *are* grateful. But there is nothing to do—no family we can safely visit, no healthy diversions beyond Netflix. Black Friday dawns bright and cold, the first truly winter day. Too dispirited to shop, even online, I propose we venture out to explore our new neighborhood, starting with The Slopes.

The South Side Slopes is eponymous, a vertiginous maze of goat-path streets and stairways clinging to the steep northern face of the mountain, Mt. Washington, that forms the river valley that is Pittsburgh. The neighborhood is paradoxical—homey and surreal, ephemeral and ancient, dense with precarious three-story frame houses, anchored by sturdy brick houses of worship. The former church in which we now live, St. Matthew's, sits at the foot of the Slopes, in the part of the South Side just as accurately called The Flats.

I do a little research and decide we'll follow the Church Route, an itinerary created by the neighborhood association highlighting four Catholic churches—St. Adalbert's, St. Michael's, St. Paul's, and St. Josaphat's—via several of the Slopes's sixty-eight sets of public stairways. Called "city steps" by Pittsburghers, they allow the citizens of our vertical metropolis to scale our landscape efficiently. For more than a century, city steps were the means by which steel workers on the Slopes got down to the riverside mills, children made it to school, and homemakers, like my immigrant grandmother, managed marketing and church.

As I plot the route, I notice how the saints' names are apostrophized when we say them but are not in the buildings' formal names. This makes sense, as the saint to whom each church is dedicated is, in fact, the parish's patron, spiritually guarding the structure and guiding its flock. The building we now live in, the former St. Matthew Catholic Church, was marketed to us as Matthew's Lofts, cleverly invoking and obscuring the presence of the Evangelist at once. A disciple of Christ, Matthew is the reputed author of the first Gospel, the bridge between the Old Testament's prophecies and the New Testament's fulfillments. He's often depicted with a pen in his hand, an apt patron, I suppose, for my husband and me, two writers seeking serenity and shelter (and central air and off-street parking) for our last third of life.

There are an astounding number of churches and religious schools on the South Side, constructed out of the faith, homesickness, desire, and sacrifice of immigrants to this city over the last two centuries. Our new home was built by Slovaks, who christened it *Kostola sv. Matúša* in 1905. By 1955, the sanctuary where we lay our heads was the spiritual home of 1500 souls. Hardly any of the ecclesiatical structures on the

South Side still fulfill their original purpose; most are now condos and apartments for unrooted families like ours. Every step we take is on desanctified ground.

St. Adalbert (956-987), Martyr

Having come north from balmy Washington, Rosalie is not fully armored for winter, but I insist she'll warm up as we go. Soon it's apparent that our body heat cannot fight the wind, which cuts our unmasked faces and penetrates our inadequate coats. My daughter, who never misses a trick, side-eyes me with mild accusation as we arrive at St. Adalbert's, an imposing red brick Romanesque edifice near the train tracks that divide the Flats from the Slopes, dwarfing the modest workers' houses around it like a feudal castle. Statues of apostles and of St. Adalbert himself, cast in moldering concrete, spy down upon us from looming bell towers, the Evangelists taking notes. Squinting back up at them, my two fellow pilgrims blow clouds of impatient breath. They are shivering, and though Adalbert's is the last functioning Roman Catholic church on the South Side—a consolidation of seven ethnic parishes, including the one that harbors our still-warm beds—its massive wooden doors are locked.

I fumble in my gloves to coax some animating information from my phone–how in 1899 pious Polish mill workers laid the cornerstone in front of us, inscribed with a verse of Psalm 83, which Google translated from the Polish as *the exiles who live in your house will praise you for centuries.*

How fitting, I say, for a church built, like all of the holy dwellings of the South Side, by exiles–the Poles, Germans, Ukrainians, Lithuanians, Serbians, Croatians, and Slovaks —seeking refuge for the rituals of their religion and the comforts of their language. My own father, a Croatian immigrant, has told me you once could walk the streets of the South Side and not hear a single word of English.

And get this, I say, literally warming to my subject. St. Adalbert, patron saint of Poland, was the first Slavic saint, martyred in the cause of Christianizing Europe. Decapitated while baptizing Prussian pagans, his holy skull is housed in Prague cathedral, where it is displayed on major feast days.

But my frozen followers have already started up the trestle steps, taking them two at a time like gazelles, and I pant after them, pointing out the fallout shelter and church auditorium (now a condo development site), the *Polska Szkoła* (Polish School, now apartments), and the convent of the Felician sisters who once taught 1200 students in Polish and English against the constant rumble and coal dust from the railroad we are now crossing over.

I know it's cold. But I start to wonder why I am the only one among us moved by this place, these rugged remnants of a one-block Polish universe, constructed brick by brick in the name of faith. None of us, it's true, has any faith, at least in the conventional sense. My husband let his lapse, as the Catholics put it, before I met him. I received a rudimentary Presbyterian formation that didn't take and which I scarcely remember. Together we raised our children without a church or even a notion of God.

Perhaps it's because, unlike my husband and my daughter, I'm the child of an immigrant, a child who watched her father's transformation, from one kind of man into another entirely, on the rare occasions when he spoke his mother tongue.

It happens that I am the descendant of *two* generations of immigrants to the South Side, and so my migration to this neighborhood is in fact a kind of return. My grandmother, an unwed mother, came in 1938 to enter an arranged marriage with a Croatian steelworker who worked at Jones and Laughlin, the mill that commanded the South Side riverfront. She left her six-year-old child behind in a village near Zagreb, and that child, my father, had to wait twenty years to see her again, finally coming to the South Side on his own in 1958 at the age of 27, the age my daughter is now.

While my grandmother stayed cloistered in her row house and church (St. George's, near the crest of Mt. Washington) and in her loveless marriage, where only Croatian was spoken, my dad had to hit the ground running. Instead of mass he went to adult education classes at South Side High School (now condos), learning enough English in a year to get a job and ask an American girl on a date. He only had enough cash and savvy to take her to the fights, a Golden Gloves match at the South Side Market House. She married him anyway.

The rest, as they say, is history—my history. I was born at South Side Hospital (now University of Pittsburgh Medical Center) in 1963, just across from St. Matthew's, and my folks, like most young people of their generation, moved over the Slopes to a greener neighborhood on the other side of the mountain. I never learned to speak Croatian because it wasn't a language my parents shared, and my father had no time, between working and learning to navigate the subtleties of our hybrid, illogical tongue, to teach us.

But I heard him speak Croatian. When he phoned his cousins at Easter, long-distance calls that required all of us to hush as he shouted across the ocean. When he argued with my grandmother and her difficult husband over the *sarma* at Christmas. And especially when he took us back to Yugoslavia, long trips my parents could barely afford, just so he could see the friends he played handball with, the aunts and uncles who took turns raising him.

Each time we went back to Zagreb, it was strange to witness his transformation. There was my father, as familiar to me as my own body, whose voice was the first sound I remember lulling me to sleep. But from that voice flowed a new pattern of notes and tones, and on his face a new set of expressions—open joy, canny delight. Even his laugh erupted more naturally, laughter pouring out of him until tears started in the corners of his eyes. It made me wonder if I'd ever truly amused him, if I'd ever really understood what he was saying.

If you've watched a person you love become a person you don't know, it's hard to put this vision into words. It's like hearing someone's singing voice for the first time. It's like seeing water turn into wine. And it helps you imagine the waves of exiles here, each trying to protect the core of who they were to themselves. I've read how in the South Side parishes, called "language" parishes by the diocese, hundreds of workers offered up their labor, their prayers, their meager wages, and their children, to create these impenetrable walls around their mother tongue.

And like motherhood itself, it worked for a time, until their children and their children scaled the walls and fled over the hills, to the open fields of America.

St. Michael, Archangel

One hundred and forty-four steps later, we're at St. Michael's on Pius St, winded but still not warmed. St. Michael's parish stretches its sooty brick length—church, rectory, parish house, school—across the middle of the Slopes like the exposed spine of a sleeping giant.

To catch my breath and stall my leggy companions, I tell them how ironic it is that this suite of buildings, the oldest on the tour, was constructed by Germans after an epidemic. Decimated by cholera in 1849, the panicked congregants of St. Michael's prayed to St. Roch, the plague saint, to intercede on their behalf. He evidently did, which is why the parish survived to erect this colossal church, its members now folded into the flock at St. Adalbert's, and why it still celebrates a Cholera Day mass on August 16, fulfilling a promise by the faithful of the Slopes to perpetually thank St. Roch for his intercession.

My daughter huffs her feigned interest. I consider whether my fun fact is ironic at all, given that we, too, live in a time of plague, of disease as constant and mercurial as the wind. From the stylish balconies and rooftop decks of St. Michael's, now a condominium development with the schmaltzy name of "Angels' Arms," the views of downtown Pittsburgh *are* celestial, though for most of its history St. Michael's muscular spire rose out of a miasma of smoke from the industry below. St. Michael is an angel himself, of course, not a human martyr, venerated by all Judeo-Christian faiths. He spoke to Moses on Mount Sinai; he battles the Devil in heaven; he leads the souls of the departed from this life and presents them to the Lord for judgment.

Which, blowing on my hands, is where I find myself. An exile from the country of work and motherhood, I have recently arrived at a kind of afterlife—life after daily lesson plans and monthly paychecks, life after my children have been raised and delivered into their own keeping. And what, I wonder, now that I have time to think about it, will be my judgment? Did I teach well? Have I been a good mother?

The woman I should ask has ducked under the arched entryway of someone's luxury apartment and is stomping her frozen feet. I remember when she nearly died in my care. At fourteen, she became mysteriously unwell, with persistent high fevers and intermittent back pain, which for an appallingly long time neither I nor any of the doctors I took her to connected as dots. I let an orthopedist send us away without examining her because he was afraid her fever was a sign of the plague of the day, H1N1. Misreading her adolescent stoicism, I waited too long to get her admitted to the hospital, where I let a radiologist bully an infectious disease specialist out of the proper kind of biopsy, delaying her diagnosis—osteomyelitis, a bacterial infection of the spine—by precious days. Unable to stop her febrile tremors, I let her take a hot shower unaccompanied, where she promptly fainted.

The list of my sins goes on, and it loops in my brain even now when I struggle to sleep. Though she ultimately recovered, the invisible infection consumed a disk in her spine before the germ and the antibiotic to stop it were identified. How she contracted it remains a mystery. My daughter's gait has a slight hitch, now, likely only noticeable to her mother walking behind her.

I am a mother walking in the knowledge that she failed to protect her child. As we slog on, up the St. Michael Street steps and towards the Monastery Street steps, I ruminate about that crisis, remembering how I wished for a god or intercessory I believed in so I could send up a prayer and release my fears. *Lord*, I hungered to say, *preserve her*. At the darkest time, while she languished before our very eyes, a panic seized me so entirely I felt I'd disappeared. Still, she suffered, and I was unable to relieve her suffering.

It is a temptation of the afterlife, this odd period of reaping and reflection after so many years of headlong sowing, to forgive myself. There may not be a soul on earth, including the lovely, healthy woman loping ahead of me, who would say I didn't try my best. But something hard in me resists the platitudes of work and love, just as I have always resisted the pieties of religion. A strength in me wants to bear the weight of my failings. It feels like the closest thing I've got to wisdom, acknowledging that I conducted myself imperfectly; I may have done real harm.

My late mother-in-law, who raised five children, was prone to ruminating in this way as long as I knew her, during thirty-five years of her afterlife as a mother. A devout Catholic, she used to say she thought God should give every mother a "disposable child," one to practice on and learn from, before she went about the terrifyingly consequential work of bringing new humans into the world. It was a metaphor, not a fantasy. She never really thought through how you'd "dispose" of this practice child. But now that she has passed and I have arrived at the precise age she was when I first met her, I understand where she was coming from—this place I stand now, evaluating the fruits of my labor and taking my own measure as a mother.

The only time I set foot in a South Side church before I lived in one was when I was asked to eulogize my grandmother, further up the hill we're perched on, at St. George's in 1999. At the time my son was just six, the age my father was when she'd placed a coin in his little palm and sent him to the movies, then vanished to America, instantly orphaning him and leaving him in the care of relatives. Once I became a mother, this story I'd heard many times shocked me anew. How could she? I mean, literally, how could you move your body away from your child and keep going?

My father was my grandmother's disposable child. She bore two more children with her new husband, and they raised those daughters here on the South Side while my father bounced among strained households in war-ravaged Yugoslavia. That day at St. George's, where she spent many hours on her knees, the business at hand was to deliver my grandmother to her final judgment, and I did not want to condemn her, nor to lie in church about who she really was, so I stammered through some vague remarks. But judge her I did, secretly. Likely her faith had by then granted her absolution in confession, but from the altar of new motherhood, I felt justified in castigating the mother she was in 1938.

But from where I stand now, long roads of decisions spool behind me, too, bringing me to just this shaky step. I consider how intimately my grandmother knew her trespasses, her own and those committed against her. The identity of my father's father was a mystery she took to her grave—a stranger passing through her rural village. I think about the deep well of fear she plunged into, crossing the Atlantic with another strange man and with the sound of her child, confused and in distress, alive in her. I have been in that well.

St. Paul of the Cross (1694-1775), Founder of the Passionist Order
Here, at the top of Mt. Washington, is where we are at last taken in. St. Paul of the Cross Church, the worship center of an active monastery of Passionist Fathers, is open. We take quiet steps into the gleaming, empty sanctuary, looking up at the gilded Corinthian columns supporting the church's brightly lit, arched firmament. On the earthly plane shine lustrous marble floors and plaques dedicated to donors for the building's recent renovation. Most of the money came in the form of a miraculous intercession by a Pittsburgh-area contractor who answered the prayers of the abbot and his dwindling band of brothers with enough material and labor to forestall closing the monastery and selling the property for (what else?) condominiums.

The heated air radiates within us, restoring everyone's mood. But what we see as we go deeper, treading softly past newly burnished bas reliefs of the Stations of the Cross, is suffering—the progression of Christ's Passion (*passio* = *suffering* in Latin), culminating in a 50-ton marble altar screen on which a monumental Jesus perishes. Standing at the foot of the Cross—where we find ourselves now—and meditating on Christ crucified, is the central tenet and practice of the Passionists, a contemplative-penitent order whose founder, Paulo Franceso Danei, taught his followers to venerate Jesus's suffering, calling it "a precious balm which sweetens all our pains." It is said that Paul, a legendary preacher, formed his devotion to suffering at his mother's knee, as she read to him from the *Lives of the Saints*.

One of my failings as a parent was an inability to convey even the simplest understanding of religious faith to my children. When my daughter was four years old, I worried that while we weren't raising our children in a church, we did celebrate the big Christian holidays, and that while they knew that Christmas was the occasion of a baby named Jesus's birth, we had not clued them in to the end of the story: his death and resurrection at Easter. Though my husband and I could not imagine childhood without the biannual delights of Santa Claus and the Easter Bunny, I was anxious for the period of fantasy and bald-faced lying to be over, so we could celebrate holidays truthfully, all of us in on the rituals and charades. In the meantime, it made no sense that Christmas was about the birth of a child and Easter was about, well, rabbits, as far as they knew. So I purchased an age-appropriate picture book, *The Easter Story* by Carol Heyer, marketed as a straightforward introduction to the Biblical story, with fine art color illustrations.

In *The Easter Story*, Heyer never shows the face of the Savior, using perspective cleverly to focus instead on his hands, as he heals the sick and turns over the cashboxes of the moneylenders in the Temple and breaks bread at the Last Supper. The crucifixion itself is described but not depicted, and the text artfully leaves out the gory details—*Pilate let the soldiers take Jesus away, and the soldiers put him on a cross. While the soldiers waited for him to die, Jesus's friends gathered around the cross, trying to comfort each other.*

I appreciated the effort this author made to deliver the Passion mildly, without the violence and pain. And I attempted to tell it that way, in the soothing storytelling voice I learned from my own mother, the one that channels the ocean of the wide world into one gentle stream of language that makes the marvelous real, the frightening safe, the strange comical, the familiar new. But my daughter was having none of it.

Put him on a cross? What does that mean?

Having never sat in a church, she did not have this image at hand. I found myself, it occurred to me, too late, having to convey literally what churches do figuratively. In a functioning Catholic church, you don't have to picture Christ on the Cross; they picture him for you, as he is here in all his gruesome glory at St. Paul's: crown of thorns, emaciated torso, feet pinned primly together with one crude stake.

With the beautiful book in my lap, I outlined for my child the simple shape of a cross, its deathly, purposeful design becoming clearer—one arm here, one arm there. I imagined all crosses from then on—tic-tac-toe, telephone poles—glowing with foul intent for her. Then I had to explain how they affixed him to this device, trying not to mention *nails*, and my storytelling voice petered out to a whisper.

Why didn't anybody help him?

For a faithful mother, this question is where you drive the lesson of the story home. You might say, as a Catholic parenting website suggests and which St. Paul of the Cross passionately encouraged: *He put up with the punishment because he loves us.*

But I didn't believe that, and I didn't want her to believe it. That this horrific death was for *her*. By that time, I had told her all kinds of stories I didn't believe a word of, of bunnies who wore jackets sewn by their mothers, of bears floating to the treetops on party balloons, but I realized all at once that this story was different. I was afraid that even if I said, "some people believe" that Jesus died for *them*, that it was an act of *love*, it might change her in a way I didn't want her to be changed.

While I was stumbling around with my answer, she turned the page, which featured the hands of a resurrected Jesus caressing the downcast head of Mary Magdalene. But one of his hands, hands familiar to us from every scene in the book, had a bright, deep gash on the back of it.

I closed the book. I said, *I'm not liking this story very much and I think we should read another one.* To which she readily agreed, sensing, I suppose, my suffering.

At the foot of the Cross I consider what, failing this simplest of tasks, I also failed to convey to my children, what principles of human understanding? Empathy, humility, gratitude? These are the guiding stars of the Passionists, the take-home philosophy of most Christian churches. What did I choose when I chose to extend the exile of my family from the house of the Lord, so far that we could no longer even decipher its language of signs and symbols?

And what business do I have, dwelling in such a house? Archly inviting my dinner guests to *six o'clock mass*? The unspeakable agony of the Passion is getting to me, or maybe I'm just a little too hot, but suddenly I'm the one who wants to split, and I pull my daughter away from the altar and towards the side aisle and exit.

Where we are arrested by a brilliant white figure, a young woman carved in blinding white porcelain, writhing on her back atop a marble tomb. The stone figure, ghostly and corporeal, has one arm raised in the air, palm facing us, as if to warn us away.

It looks like she's being raped, Rosalie says, and I stifle my startled laugh to shush her. There's no plaque or sign to tell us what we're seeing, or even who donated the money for the tomb—or is it a shrine? Ruing again my own ignorance of religious iconography, I bluff. It's probably Mary Magdalene or the Blessed Mother herself, I reassure her, grieving at the foot of the Cross.

St. Maria Goretti (1890-1902), Martyr

Three-hundred winding steps down, through the spiraling bones of invasive vines and the tidy hopes of the frosted kitchen gardens of the tenacious denizens of the Slopes, we're back on Pius Street, where we pause. Here, at the top of the 18th Street steps, we have a decision to make: turn right towards the last church on the tour, St. Josaphat's (now being developed as apartments and a "Wellness Marketplace," whatever that is), or descend this last cascade straight back down to St. Matthew's, whose graceful green steeple we spy beneath us. One of the recurring benefits of living in a church is that you always have a compass to guide you home.

Though I want to see the church of St. Josaphat, martyr (1580-1623), hacked to death in the cause of reunifying Polish Catholics with the Roman rite church, my traveling companions have had enough. So I make a deal: listen to the remarkable story of St. Maria Goretti, glowing urgently in my palm, and we can skip St. Joe's and go back to our own damned church for lunch.

You know where this is going. Maria Goretti, claimed by the Passionists as a saint of their own order, is the tormented woman we just saw in St. Paul's. Only she wasn't a woman at all. At eleven years old, the youngest canonized saint of the Catholic Church achieved her martyrdom by, as my daughter correctly surmised, fending off a rapist and dying at his hands.

In an impoverished Italian village in 1902, Maria Goretti was left at home to watch her two younger siblings while her widowed mother went out into the fields to thresh fava beans. Alessandro Serenelli, a twenty-year-old neighbor with whom Maria's family shared a house, took advantage of Maria's vulnerable position to attempt, not for the first time, to violate her. With her right arm, the one we saw raised in St. Paul's, she successfully repelled him, which enraged Serenelli, who stabbed her fourteen times with an ice pick, then returned to his side of the house to nap. The cries of her neglected baby sister brought her mother from the fields, and Maria was taken to the hospital, where she lingered long enough to be anointed by the local Passionist priest and to famously forgive Alessandro with her dying breath: "I want him to be with me in heaven."

Alessandro went to prison unremorseful, but after years in solitary confinement he had a dream in which Maria appeared to him, offering fourteen white lilies—one for each of the wounds he inflicted upon her. This vision triggered his conversion and is considered Maria Goretti's first miracle. Upon his release from prison, Serenelli testified repeatedly to the "purity" of Maria in the wildly popular and urgent case for her canonization as a patroness of chastity and forgiveness.

That canonization occurred on June 24, 1950, in front of an unprecedented audience of 500,000 in St. Peter's Square, the first rock-star canonization. Living long enough to witness both Maria's martyrdom and her ascension to sainthood were Alessandro himself and Maria's mother, Assunta—a mother, if there ever was one, who failed to protect her child, yet who ultimately forgave and befriended her daughter's killer. My own grandmother may have lit a candle to the doomed girl in her spotless South Side kitchen and watched her glorification on television.

God, I'm glad you never took us to church, says my daughter, shuddering, and, at last, impressed.

I could take some satisfaction in this. There's an interior scorecard in every parent, I suspect, that draws us to scour our children's adult selves for points. But I don't feel vindicated in my decision not to raise my daughter in a religion, or even largely responsible for the earnest, ethical woman she has in fact become. Trained in diplomacy, she's building a career as a public servant. Though I heartily approve of her path, every step she's taken away from me since the time she could walk has been her own idea. It may be the only miracle I believe in, that my children formed themselves in their own images, in spite of my flawed care. It makes me think about my own father and what a wonder he must have seemed when he appeared to his mother after twenty years of exile, fully grown, as good and gentle a man who ever walked the earth.

Skipping stairs down to our own little church, following my own tiny tribe, I continue to wonder about the interior weather of those who truly live in the bosom of the Mother Church, not simply inhabit her buildings. In just one day's excursion, I've felt both the heat of the Passion and the chill of a theology that values women for their purity and forgives men for, well, everything. I think about my own grandmother, who endured a censured motherhood and a miserable but sanctified marriage. I also think about my mother-in-law, who found courage in praying the Rosary, enough to muscle through decades of marital and maternal doubt. It must be complicated to navigate, this faith, this labyrinth of comfort and shame, of hope and dread, of soothing ritual and troubling mortification. Though promised very specific heavenly rewards, you might have a hard time picturing the earthly life you truly deserve.

It certainly isn't cool, or edgy, or funny—the things people say about what it must be like to live in a church. It's relentless, is what I come to, finally, passing my key fob over the remote-control door lock. Relentless—this wind, this need for shelter, this hunger for direction, this desire for benediction. Have I done good? Have I worked well? How much happiness do I deserve? I may be asking these questions here in my sliver of a South Side sanctuary, coolly minimalist and stripped of its sacred adornments, for all the rest of my days.

Given her profession and the nature of her own seeking, my daughter may extend her exile even farther, like her brother has in Brazil. Both of my children may forgo not just their motherland but motherhood or fatherhood entirely. In my darker hours, I wonder if there's *any* place on the diseased planet they have inherited that looks to them like a promised land.

Perhaps this is a natural cycle. Waves of departure and arrival may be the most permanent feature of the American landscape, especially Pittsburgh's. Its industrial age, which drew the immigrants from eastern Europe from whom I have doubly descended, was a century-long tide that has long receded. The newest wave brings swells of professionals from every part of the world to our research universities and healthcare conglomerates, exiles who are remaking the landscape to suit their needs and desires. My own unscientific research on the subject reveals that wine fridges, stainless steel oven hoods, and granite countertops are the icons of their faith.

But what do I know? Here in my last third of life, there's still so much to figure out, and I write in the only faith I possess, which is that it's worthwhile to wonder. I don't know if I'll ever come full circle to become, like my grandmother, a grandmother on the South Side of Pittsburgh. I don't know if I've earned even one of the tender mercies arrayed before me now—my daughter's cheeks flushing over a cup of steaming soup, my husband fiddling with the fancy new thermostat—all of us at home, at last and for the moment, agreeably trembling from our exertions. But I accept them as such, as blessings. I shall praise them forever.

That Good Night

NANCY GRACE MCCABE

In June 2020, my brother Jeff texts me, asking me to contribute money to clean up the jungle-like lot in Wichita where our childhood home sits. "Shouldn't we just have the house torn down?" I ask.

I imagine walking through it one last time. I picture the curio shelf, the big fireplace and piano and bookshelves crammed with yellow-bordered *National Geographics*, even though I know that the reality is moldy, rotted floors, filthy bathrooms with sagging shower doors, gnawed corners and mouse droppings.

Jeff says that tearing it down will cost at least $10,000. He can't afford it yet. Maybe in a few months.

The house was abandoned years ago after repeatedly flooding when the city widened the highway. But I still feel irrationally ashamed about the overgrown lot, the deteriorating house, exasperated at my family's failure to maintain appearances. We forget to mow our lawns, we let weeds take over, we leave behind lost causes like my hopelessly damaged childhood home. I envy people whose gardens bloom with casual artfulness behind sturdy houses with uncluttered granite countertops, stylish squishy furniture, and polished but substantial antiques. I envy people who live long lives, unlike my dad, who should have gone to the doctor sooner, unlike my mom who became so consumed by grief that she let her own health decline. Other people appear impervious, disguise decay, defy time. Not my family.

A couple of weeks after Jeff's text, my younger brother Bob calls. Jeff's boss just contacted him; Jeff didn't return to work after a vacation. I realize that I haven't seen any Facebook updates from him in a while, either.

"He's probably in a hotel room somewhere, too sick to get home," I say, but I'm uneasy. Jeff can be unreliable and disorganized, but he never misses work. Top of FormBottom of Form

My own life is imperfect but basically orderly. I find clutter depressing. I pay bills on time. I make lists and check off tasks. Jeff is sloppy and spontaneous. There's a rumor that he has storage units all across America, leaving behind things when he moves and never retrieving them. On more than one occasion, he has disappeared, stranded in a hotel in eastern Kansas with congestive heart failure, immobilized by gout in Arizona, falling off the radar while visiting Colorado. His friends sounded alarms till he resurfaced, posting on Facebook, sounding mildly irritated, that he was fine.

Now my calls are bumped to Voicemail. I send a group message to the people he interacts with most on Facebook.

Uche saw Jeff eleven days ago. "He looked bad, really terrible," says Uche. "He'd put on weight. He was retaining water. I said, 'Jeff, stop trying to live like a young man. We're not young anymore.' He was always on the road, going everywhere. It wasn't good for him."

"He looked fine," says Doug, who'd seen him the next day. "He had a little cough, but that was all."

Jeff's boss dispatches an employee to his house. The employee reports back: there are three cars in the driveway, a locked garage. Mail overflowing the box, packages piled on the porch. A garbage can by the curb, full of water.

Now I'm really worried. I call the Tulsa police to request a welfare check. All goes silent for two hours. I can't stand waiting. I push redial. I'm transferred three times. When I finally reach the officer, he pauses, sounds awkward. "I'm sorry to have to tell you this," he says, "but your brother is deceased." The officer tells me that they found him on the living room floor. His body has been sent to the medical examiner's office.

My boyfriend Steve does most of the driving to Tulsa while I'm on the phone with probate attorneys and funeral homes and the medical examiner's office, trying to get results from Jeff's COVID test so we know what precautions to take. It's negative. I'm relieved. From the back seat, my daughter Sophie makes us a reservation at an Air B&B.

I stare out the window, wondering what I could have done to save my brother, a futile line of thought that I can't stop following. I've tried to save people before. Like the Fourth of July when I called relentlessly looking for someone to repair my parents' broken central air, worried about the misery of my sick dad in the heat. Someone came to fix it. Within a month, my dad still died. When my mom refused to eat, I drove to the mall for a pretzel that I knew she wouldn't be able to resist. She still died days later. By now I should understand that when every choice starts to feel like a miscalculation, a mistake, I'm up against forces bigger than myself. Yet I was secretly, irrationally angry at them for succumbing too willingly to death without any burning or raving or raging. If they'd just tried hard enough, I sometimes thought, they wouldn't have died.

I will write an obituary and eulogy that will neaten up Jeff's life. Not mention things like how much he hated school, how teachers complained that he was lazy and withdrawn and uncooperative. How his weight fluctuated wildly as he grew to be 6'4". How the year we overlapped in high school, as he traveled stalwart through the halls with his pack of friends, I cringed at slick boys with loud voices whose taunts floated behind him. I kept a low profile. I'd been targeted by a similar group of boys in junior high and didn't want to repeat that. Sometimes I thought that my brother and I saw in each other reflections of our own awkward weirdness and avoided each other because of it.

My family had always seen me as the self-sufficient one. I was six months old when my nineteen-month-old brother contracted a rare blood disease. Mom abruptly weaned me and farmed me out to relatives while she spent nights at the hospital. When they built our house, my parents carpeted the room next to theirs in blue and papered it with brightly colored sailboats, balloons, and trucks. For me, they installed pink carpet and wallpaper flecked with gold and pink in the furthest away bedroom. Now I look back at the messages of architecture and décor: that I was expected to be a small if feminine adult at three, that four-year-old brother was a little boy who still needed them.

But I was always glad to have the room with the most privacy. While Jeff remained sickly, I grew up robustly healthy, logging perfect school attendance. My family disapproved of me for seemingly having things easy and yet still being discontent enough to complain, to chafe at restrictions, to be the first to leave home, to depart sharply from their conservative worldview. Nevertheless Mom was inordinately pleased that I kept a tidy house, ate salads, dutifully had my brakes fixed and my teeth cleaned, and saved for retirement.

Of course I won't include any of this in my eulogy. Instead, I'll talk about the video footage that suggests that as babies and toddlers Jeff and I were best friends: he assists me as I take my first wobbly steps, we sit together criss-cross applesauce watching *Romper Room*. I will mention how my brother always arrived when he felt like it and not a moment before.

I will mention his gruff voice, his ready laugh, his ironic sense of humor.

A day and a half after leaving Pennsylvania, we pull up to the curb outside Jeff's house. Bob and some cousins have arrived ahead of us. It looks like they're holding a garage sale, furniture spread out across the driveway. "It smelled pretty bad," says my cousin Bill. "We just wanted to get it out of the house." The probate attorney said not to remove anything, but really? We should leave trash and cat feces, rags of old clothing, heaps of mail, boxes that were never unpacked after my brother moved here five years ago, a garage full of more boxes that seem to have come from a recently emptied storage unit?

I'm flooded by a sense of shame. I have a vague memory of refusing to enter the bathroom downstairs after Jeff moved to the house's lower level in his teens. The toilet had repeatedly clogged, overflowed, and leaked until the floor was permanently damaged. Mom gave up on the spaces where my brother lived. She just closed the doors. The whole time I'm in Tulsa, I simply won't enter those bathrooms. I'll drive to a convenience store down the street to pee.

The central air in the house broke a few years ago and apparently Jeff never had it repaired. It's 90 degrees outside and in here the heat is suffocating. My shock and shame renew themselves: how did my brother function in this stifling air? How did he sleep? He made a decent salary, had cars, a camper, a motorcycle, guns, but doesn't seem to have called a plumber, didn't replace the air conditioning unit, didn't mow the back lawn. In the sweltering kitchen, cousins have sorted hundreds of unopened envelopes into piles across the table and counters. I feel at once judgmental and embarrassed and horrified and apologetic, as if my biggest failure is not having somehow saved my brother from living like this.

Jeff's friend Doug, an attorney, drives to Tulsa to help me sort papers. In the oppressive heat of the living room, Doug says, "How did he live like this? No wonder he liked to visit me in Wichita. We even referred to the guest room as 'Jeff's room.'" And then, mournfully, "Was he so ill that he just didn't have the energy to take care of things? How did I not know that?" He shakes his head, eyes roving the room, as if he didn't really know my brother, his best friend, after all. As if he had failed him somehow. "I didn't know," he kept saying. "I just didn't know. And you know him. He deflected. He was never serious. If you got too close to the truth, he deflected."

Later I talk to Jeff's other best friend, Uche, on the phone. "I'm not that shocked," he says when I tell him about the state of things. "We used to be roommates. Jeff was just always a mess." Later in the conversation, his voice is full of sadness as he says, "He was a lonely guy."

Guilt and remorse and sorrow stab through me, as if there's something I could have done to change that. In the long silence as Doug looks around my brother's living room, in the long pause on the phone with Uche, I can almost hear them thinking the same thing.

The funeral home feels hushed, solemn and serious. Bob and I are ushered to a room with comfy chairs, discreetly placed Kleenex, and gravestone and vault plaques on the walls. They are all for someone named Mary C. Matthews, advertisements for the ways we can memorialize our loved one. On one plaque she was born in 1960 and in another 1943. She was a beloved wife, mother, and daughter. She was an accomplished engineer. She was an inspiring English teacher. A talented dancer. A gourmet cook. There are a dozen versions of Mary C. Matthews.

I look at the plaques and I think of the dozens of versions of my brother. The one who made terrible grades but much higher ACT scores than I did and 100 percent in a college chemistry class I barely passed. The extrovert with many friends who was isolated, especially during the pandemic. The one with whom I had long, funny texting conversations that brought us closer during the last few years after decades in which we'd had no relationship.

When we were teenagers, when Jeff lived downstairs and I lived upstairs, I went to school during the day and he worked nights. In our twenties, I'd come home for visits and barely see him. I'd go downstairs for a late night snack and run into his friends in the kitchen. "Who are you?" they'd ask, and I'd say, "I'm Jeff's sister," and they'd look blank. They hadn't known he had a sister.

For three days, we sort through mail and boxes and items, looking for a will that doesn't exist, locating valuables, renting a dumpster to dispose of trash, and arranging for cremation and a probate process. I flip through the paintings that were hanging on the wall of the room where my brother died. My dad once collected forty-some of these clichéd landscapes that used to make me feel embarrassed about my family's taste and even more embarrassed by my own snobbery. Now I keep three of them.

Despite a thousand pieces of unopened mail, a houseful of flashlights and clocks, of laptops and exercise equipment, of sock monkey magnets and coins passed down by my grandpa and a ring passed from oldest son to oldest son ever since the first McCabe arrived from Ireland, I'm still trying to figure out how to summarize my brother in a eulogy. We had so little in common: him with his TV shows, guns, cars, motorcycles, electronics, road trips, Jimmy Buffet songs, me with my books and piano, folk music, beaches, walks and bike rides, dance. And yet even during the years we barely communicated, Mom pointed out that independently, while living in different states, Jeff and I bought the same couch and ocean-themed shower curtain. And once we discovered that our handwriting looked creepily alike.

So our relationship was never a lost cause even when there seemed little to salvage. Once in our thirties, Jeff came to visit me in South Carolina. He arrived two days after his projected ETA, went straight to bed, and didn't stir until 3 p.m. the next day. He declined to stay for dinner and was on his way at 6 p.m., embarking on a ten-hour drive back to Ohio. Maybe we were both nervous that we'd have nothing to talk about. And yet over the years I learned, especially through Facebook, that we had similar ironic senses of humor and appreciation for quirky tourist attractions and impatience with racism and homophobia and social rankings and petty meanness.

After our parents died, he said to me, "We need to make an effort to stay in touch and get together for holidays." I offered to cook him a Cornish game hen every Christmas, but he never showed up. Once he drove all the way from Kansas to San Diego to see Sophie compete at YMCA Gymnastics Nationals, arriving in the middle of her final event. After his heart surgery, I invited him to recover at my house. He seemed pleased by the offer, but he didn't follow up.

I organize a virtual memorial service, deliver my unsatisfactory eulogy. The medical examiner's report comes back, designating heart disease as the cause of death. Eventually, I locate one of my brother's storage units, in Ohio. Steve and I sort through clothes, photos, tools, tents with missing pieces, fishing poles, a 20-year-old two-pound bag of walnuts. And boxes and bags full of loose and rolled coins and coin albums and proof sets and unused rolling papers. I examine a roll labelled "wash quarters." I assume they were intended for my brother's laundry.

I'm on my way to the Walmart Coinstar machine with boxes of change when I remember my dad shaking coins out of his pockets every evening, picking through them, looking for copper and silver, wheat pennies and mercury dimes. It strikes me that Jeff would have never been patient and methodical enough to roll these coins. When our dad died, Jeff must have brought these back to Ohio, and then, when he was abruptly transferred, tossed everything into a storage unit with rental fees he went on paying for twenty years. Through Google, I discover that the *wash quarters* are Washington quarters with high silver content.

Even though this family legacy sat in a storage unit for twenty years, I feel guilty turning it over to a coin dealer. He sorts through the collection and presents me with a check for $10,000.

I think about the fictional Mary C. Matthews, imagining alternate universes in which the same person can play out multiple lives. I imagine my brother alive in some alternate universe, because how is it possible to die like this at the age of 58? We should have grown old, reminiscing about our childhoods in our 80s. Instead I'm stuck with the job of raging against the light on behalf of everyone else.

And suddenly it occurs to me that Dylan Thomas's famous villanelle isn't so much about nobly fighting the inevitable forces of mortality. It's about denial. Because denial makes us feel better, like we have some control.

In the winter, I have my childhood home demolished. Afterward, my cousin Melinda Facetimes me from the edge of Greenwich Road next to what used to be our driveway. The camera pans a wide blur of treeless, houseless, snow-patched land. No chimney, swingset, porch, metal shed, pigeon pen, grapevines, apple tree. All gone, with no sign now of machinery, dumpsters, hardhats, debris. I feel a hollow sense of loss and inadequacy and regret.

Later, I stare at the paintings I've hung in my upstairs rooms: A lighthouse in stormy weather. A gothic house perched on a cliff above the sea, windows lighted. A pond with a waterwheel attached to a wooden house. Simple, ordinary lives within walls that will never crumble.

And even though I know there's little I could have done to save my brother or my childhood home, I feel stricken, the question still lingering: what if I gave up too easily?

CONTRIBUTORS

Lauren Abunassar is an Arab-American journalist and writer. She holds graduate degrees from NYU and the Iowa Writers' Workshop and her work has appeared in *LA Magazine, Salon, The Offing, Narrative, Poetry,* and elsewhere. Her first book is forthcoming from University of Arkansas Press this fall as the recipient of the Etel Adnan poetry prize.

Marc Blanc is a Ph.D. candidate in American literature at Washington University in St. Louis. His research traces an interracial history of leftist publishing in the Midwest during its boom years, 1877–1945.

Ed Breen *has been an Indiana journalist for 50 years. He was a reporter, photographer and editor at the Marion Chronicle Tribune from 1966-1995, when he became Assistant Managing Editor of the Journal Gazette newspaper in Fort Wayne.*

Demetrius A. Buckley *is a poet and creative writer. His work has been published in The Michigan Quarterly Review, RHINO, Mangoprism, Filter, The Arkana Journal and Apogee. He's working on a memoir: First 48: The Fall of Winter Kings and is the 2021 Toi Derricotte & Cornelius Eady Chapbook Prize winner for his poetry collection Here is Home. He is serving a 20- to 32-year sentence for a second degree murder at Michigan Reformatory (RMI).*

Matthew Chasney *is a Cleveland-based photographer. He is team oriented, has great attention to detail and is proficient in the Microsoft suite.*

Emma Cieslik *(she/her) is a queer museum professional and religious scholar researching the intersections between gender, sexuality, material culture, and religion.*

Avery Gregurich is a writer living and working in Marengo, Iowa. He was raised next to the Mississippi River and has never strayed too far from it.

Eileen G'Sell *is a poet and culture critic with recent contributions to The Baffler, Fence, Oversound, The Hopkins Review, Current Affairs, Hyperallergic, Reverse Shot, LARB, and other outlets. Her first full-length volume of poetry, Life After Rugby, was published in 2018 by Gold Wake Press, and she is a 2023 nominee for the Rabkin Foundation award in arts journalism. She teaches at Washington University in St. Louis.*

Robert Isenberg *is a freelance writer, playwright, photographer, stage performer, and documentary filmmaker. He is a past recipient of the Brickenridge Fellowship, McDowell Scholarship, Trespass Residency, and two Golden Quill Awards. He earned his MFA in Creative Writing from Chatham University, where he served as Whitford Fellow, the program's highest honor. Originally from Vermont, he lived in Pittsburgh for 16 years. For two years he lived in Costa Rica, where he served as a staff writer for The Tico Times. He freelances widely and teaches for numerous institutions, including Arizona State University. Robert was recently named the newest contributing editor for Providence Monthly. He is now based in his native New England.*

Lori Jakiela is the author of four books, including the memoir *Belief Is Its Own Kind of Truth,* Maybe (2016), which received the 2016 Saroyan Prize, was a finalist for the Council of Literary Magazines and Small Presses Firecracker Award and the Housatonic Book Award, and was named one of twenty Not-to-Miss Nonfiction Books of 2015 by *The Huffington Post.* She directs the undergraduate writing program at the University of Pittsburgh at Greensburg, where she is a professor of English and Creative/Professional Writing.

Hannah Allman Kennedy grew up among the oil ghost towns of Venango County, PA. She is the author of *And It All Came Tumbling Down,* which was awarded Book of the Year at the 2023 Writer's Conference of Northern Appalachia. She lives and teaches writing in Pittsburgh, and can be found online at hannahakwrites.com

Kristin Kovacic *is author of the essay collection, History of My Breath, and the poetry chapbook House of Women, and she is editor of the anthology, Birth: A Literary Companion.She has taught English and creative writing at the Pittsburgh High School for the Performing Arts and Winchester Thurston School, as well as in the graduate writing programs of Chatham and Carlow universities. She lives on the South Side of Pittsburgh.*

Miles MacClure *is an artist and occasional writer based in Chicago. He is currently a Visual Arts Teaching Fellow at the University of Chicago, where he teaches classes on social media performance as an artform.*

Nicholas Mainieri's *debut novel, The Infinite, was a finalist for the 2017 Crook's Corner Book Prize while also being named among the best books of 2016 by Southern Living Magazine, Writer's Bone, and WBUR's On Point Radio. He studied English at the University of Notre Dame and holds an MFA from the University of New Orleans.*

Noelle Mateer is a writer in Pittsburgh. Her work appears in *Wired, Defector, The Economist* and more, and she currently writes for the *Pittsburgh Union Progress,* the publication of striking *Post-Gazette* workers.

Nancy McCabe directs the writing program at the University of Pittsburgh at Bradford and teaches in the low residency MFA program at the Spalding University School of Creative and Professional Writing. She is the author of four previous books of nonfiction and a novel. She lives in Bradford, Pennsylvania.

Taylor Michael *is an arts and culture writer with publications both forthcoming and in All Arts, Artsy, The New York Times, Belt Magazine, Hyperallergic, and The Observer. She is an adjunct professor of freshman writing at the New Jersey Institute of Technology and an associate editor at the literary magazine A Public Spaces.*

Anjulie Rao is a journalist and critic covering the built environment.

Emma Riva is the managing editor of *UP,* an international online and print magazine that covers the intersections of graffiti, street art and fine arts. She is also the author of *Night Shift in Tamaqua, an* illustrated novel set in the Lehigh Valley. She lives in Pittsburgh, PA.

Rachel Rosolina is an essayist with pieces in Still: The Journal, Women of Appalachia, Vessel Press, and more. With a bachelor's degree in English from Berea College and an MFA in creative nonfiction from West Virginia University, Rosolina now lives in Bloomington, Indiana. After more than a decade in publishing, she works remotely as communications director for Appalshop, an Eastern Kentucky media and arts nonprofit centered around amplifying and preserving Appalachian voices.

Eva Rosenfeld is a writer and artist from Michigan.

Patrick Shea was a environmental reporter at Interlochen Public Radio. Before joining IPR, he worked a variety of jobs in conservation, forestry, prescribed fire and trail work. He earned a degree in natural resources from Northland College in Ashland, Wisconsin, and his interest in reporting grew as he studied environmental journalism at the University of Montana's graduate school.

Ed Simon is the editor of *Belt Magazine.*

Ashley Stimpson is freelance journalist based in Baltimore, Maryland. Read more of her work at www.ashleystimpson.com.

Casey Taylor is an Appalachian phenotype who writes in Pittsburgh, Pennsylvania, where he lives and works with his family. He has written for Defector Media, The New Republic, WIRED, and New York Magazine's Intelligencer, among other, and also writes a folklore newsletter called Weed Church on substack. Casey is currently working on a book about cannabis, The Cold War, and His Imperial Majesty Haile Selassie.

Adria R. Walker *is a narrative reporter, whose work has appeared in The Guardian US, USA Today, Scalawag Mag and other publications. Originally from Mississippi, she has spent the last several years in Western New York. With over a decade of journalistic experience and a deep appreciation for history, Adria aims to help shed light on untold or lesser known stories. You can find her on Twitter at @adriawalkr.*